MASTERING MARKETING

Leading a Journey of Becoming

A BUSINESS DEVELOPMENT ROAD MAP

John H. Watson

Cover Image: Pixhook at iStockphoto.com
Cover Design: Jade Stevens and John Watson
Book Design: John Watson and Jade Stevens
Editor: Carol McFarlane

Published by Accrue Performance Marketing Inc.
Calgary, Alberta Canada
403-512-3183 ext. 111
AccrueMarketing.com

For additional copies or bulk orders of this book, contact sales@accruemarketing.com

First Edition

ISBN: 978-0-9813426-1-0	Trade Paper
ISBN: 978-0-9813426-6-5	Hardcover
ISBN: 978-0-9813426-2-7	ePub
ISBN: 978-0-9813426-5-8	Mobi

Categories
1. Marketing for Small Businesses 2. Small Business & Entrepreneurship 3. Marketing

FREE MARKETING RESOURCES

Want to learn more about marketing for free? John offers 18 free eBooks on his website. The eBooks were prepared for small business owners, not marketing experts or practitioners.

The eBooks cover a wide range of subjects. But they are all written to structure how you think about and approach an aspect of your marketing, rather than how to complete a task.

The goal is to help you understand your needs, before you seek help.

Download them all for free at:

https://accruemarketing.com/free-marketing-downloads/

DEDICATION

This book is for my parents, John and Sharon Watson. You were my inspiration for setting out on this quest. You role modelled self-directed learning; devouring books and putting learning into practise. I've done my best to follow your example.

I'm also dedicating this work to all the business owners and marketing directors I've worked with over the years. I'm not sure who taught whom more. Your passion and endless dedication, grit and grace inspire me as a person and as a leader.

Thank you to my wife, Laura, whose patience I have tested with my dedication to this work. I appreciate all your support. Thank you also to Carol McFarlane and Kathy Filipowitz for being my right and left hands over the last 13 years.

Thank you to Jim Freeman and Gloria Stewart who mentored me and brought me into the industry from entirely different but complementary perspectives.

As an avid learner and reader, I acknowledge the hundreds of authors, coaches, and teachers who've shaped my thinking and whose foundation I've built upon.

FOREWARD

My career as a marketing and advertising consultant spans over 45 years. I was president of Freeman Yipp Palmer Jarvis, which is now BBDO Canada, as well as the sole owner of Powerlines Strategic Marketing and Communications.

Throughout my career I worked with companies of all sizes, from the Fortune 500 to mom and pop startups and everything in between.

In particular, I found the small to mid-sized businesses struggled with marketing the most. They rarely employed in-house marketing executives due to their small marketing budgets. This left it up to the owner or sales manager to direct their marketing investments.

When these leaders hired me, they were usually driven by-pressure to perform, because they needed instant sales. As a result, they focused on expensive advertising and promotional campaigns to solve their problems. This focus was often risky. They frequently discovered, after the fact, that their margins were insufficient to cover their cost of sales from advertising. A lack of preparation often made matters worse.

To compensate, I guided my clients through a detailed strategic planning process. The process was challenging for clients because it was often their first time approaching their business from their customers' point of view.

I see the same intent in John Watson's book *Mastering Marketing*. This book guides owners of small and medium-sized business through a comprehensive strategic planning and systems development process.

When I mentored John in his early years, I would always tell him, "Marketing is everything you do to grow a business". He's clearly applied this big-picture and systematic approach in this book.

Mastering Marketing goes far beyond the classic definition of marketing. It looks to guide the entire marketing, sales and business development process in what I always called a "soup to nuts" or "start to finish approach".

I recommend *Mastering Marketing* to any business owner who's willing to do the work necessary to grow their business.

If you're looking for a thoughtful, step-by-step guide to marketing and business development, you'll find yourself returning to this book over and over, as you reach new milestones or obstacles to overcome.

Jim Freeman
President
Powerlines Strategic Marketing and Communications

ABOUT THE AUTHOR

John Watson is the President of Accrue Performance Marketing Inc., which he founded in 2006. John has over 25 years' experience serving in the role of consultant, marketing coach, and virtual chief marketing officer. He loves helping business owners grow companies.

John has worked with a wide range of industries including all manner of professional service firms, charities, private health clinics, technology companies, manufacturers, distributors, retailers, web businesses, artisans, tourism operators, natural resource companies, speakers and trainers, real estate developers, builders, and more.

John has a passion for multi-disciplinary learning, a love of nature, photography, gardening and writing. He's also a sports bike and high-performance computer enthusiast.

John lives in Calgary, Canada with his wife, Laura, and his golden retriever, Zoe.

CONTENTS

THE
INTRODUCTION

Framing for Mastering Marketing

INTRODUCTION

I became an intrapreneur in the mid 1990's when I was just a few years out of university.

I was working in an environmental engineering company, starting up a new department. I needed to learn to market and sell to get clients for myself and my team.

Keen to prove myself, I read everything I could get my hands on about sales, marketing and business development.

Unfortunately, everything I read seemed to focus on some tip, tactic, or technology out of context with any big picture. I could not see how all the pieces fit together. It left me frustrated and uncertain.

Unable to make sense of all the disconnected advice I was receiving, I wanted a map of the big picture. I wanted to see how all the pieces fit together as a system to drive earnings growth.

In my search for a map, I sought expert advice. I interviewed marketing agencies. I interviewed other entrepreneurs. I took sales training. I hired a 20-year veteran salesperson to mentor me and then I engaged business coaches, and on and on.

Despite my best efforts, I could not find a map or my way. All I could find was fragmented advice, random tips, and sales pitches on the latest fads and tactics.

It was maddening. I kept thinking, People have been building companies for hundreds of years; surely, someone must have created a map.

Eventually, I realised if I wanted a map, I needed to create one for myself, like the explorers David Thompson or Lewis and Clark.

Over the last 25+ years, my exploration and mapping efforts have undergone dozens of revisions, reorganisations, and revelations. What started as flow charts and swim lane diagrams, ultimately morphed into its current form: a 20-step leadership framework.

The Core Idea

When I could not find a suitable map, I started looking for other frameworks for inspiration. I learned about The Way of the Warrior, the Seven Virtues of Bushido, and then the Eight-Fold Paths in Buddhism that lead to enlightenment. I learned about Benjamin Franklin's 13 virtues, which he believed to be his path to success.

I had a eureka moment. My map could be a set of intentions or Ways to live into.

The premise was simple. Each intention or Way would be purposeful. Each Way would ask you to focus on why, before how. Knowing why would encourage you to evaluate options and determine where a task best fit into your priority sequence.

By sequencing the Ways into a natural, logical order, you'd have a mental map of marketing to follow. When you look at the Ways of Being as a whole, you can see how everything fits together to form a system.

There are no tricks, gimmicks, or short cuts. Rather than the endless stream of distractions, you and your team can focus on building a functional marketing system.

Learning the Ways is not unlike learning to play a musical instrument or practising a martial art. The 20 Ways are patterns and practices you live into as an individual or a company. Each Way builds upon the last to help you align with who your clients need you to be while decreasing the obstacles inhibiting growth.

The Ways of Being keep you focused on what you have the most control over: yourself and your business practices. How you choose to live into each Way will evolve to fit your environment and resources.

With this book, I aim to share the 20 Ways that have shaped the last 25+ years of my life. The Ways are the map I continue to follow on my business development journey. They are also the backbone of my coaching and consulting practice.

I hope *Mastering Marketing* helps you find your way in your business development journey. Bon Voyage.

MAKING THE SHIFT

In my experience as a sales and marketing consultant, the bane of my existence is what I have come to call "random acts of marketing".

It is safe to say it drives me crazy when I see it, and I see it everywhere.

What Are Random Acts of Marketing?

Random acts of marketing are the ineffective practices of purchasing or engaging in marketing tactics without a clear sense of purpose or clarity on how they're intended to contribute.

If you don't know how a marketing activity will contribute to your objectives, you're engaged in random acts of marketing.

In my experience, random acts of marketing are more the norm than the exception. Ask 100 small business owners about the purpose of their website or why they're investing in social media. Ask them how the investments are meant to contribute to their bottom line or how they'll measure the return on investment (ROI).

You're likely to get several blank stares and some "Gee, I'm not sure" answers.

Ask them the same question about advertising, sponsorships, networking, SEO, video marketing, app development, and just about any marketing tactic you can think of, and you'll get similar responses. "I'm not sure."

You might defend the business owners and say they're doing what their marketing people advised them to do.

Go ask the same questions of their marketing people and see if you get different answers. You're likely to get the same "uhms" and "aws" from them.

Unfortunately, marketing rationales are often driven more by trends and personal interests, than by specific business objectives.

Fortunately, you can break from this reactionary approach to marketing. You can choose to lead with a purposeful and systematic approach, focused on developing customer relationships and an earnings-growth agenda.

How Do You Do It?

You make the shift by reconsidering how you approach marketing investments.

It comes down asking a few simple questions.

1. Why are we considering this marketing activity?
2. What role is it meant to serve within our system?
3. Is there another part of our system that needs attention first?
4. Is it a fit for us, or are we forcing it?
5. What's it going to take to make it work?
6. How will we know if it's working or not?

If you can't answer these questions, hold off until you can.

WHAT IS MARKETING?

Let's start with some core ideas. The first is, marketing is not about you. It's about facilitating the needs of your customers as they journey through your business.

I'm not saying you and your brand are not important; they clearly are. The real problem is that people don't care about you or your products until they decide you're relevant to them.

Many of us start marketing by describing who we are and what we offer. Then the marketing falls flat. Why? Because you need to address the relevance gap first. You need to start with "What's in it for me?" from the buyer's perspective.

I would, however, encourage you to expand this idea to the entire customer journey. "What's in this relationship for me?" might be a next step way of thinking.

The job of marketing is not simply to help you look good but to define the shape and nature of your relationship with your clients over time. The job is to help you define "What's in this relationship for me?" in a way that maximises the lifetime value for you. We can upgrade the question again to "What's in this relationship for us?"

Given the long-term and vital nature of marketing, it's important to recognise it for what it is. It's a process to be set up and optimised, not a series of independent promotional activities.

If you accept this definition of marketing, then marketing is about building a machine or like a relationship-building assembly line.

Assembly lines are very effective in manufacturing. In fact, they changed our world in less than 100 years.

This high-speed semi-automated assembly line-approach to relationship building is a central goal of modern marketing.

What's exciting is you don't have to be some giant firm to do it. The approach and the technologies involved are accessible to small business owners. The only thing holding you back is your understanding of marketing, and how you approach it.

This is great news because you're the person you have the most control over.

If you set a new intention for marketing and live into that possibility, you can transform your company. It can become something you never imagined.

Defining Your Marketing System

Think of marketing as choreographing your customers' experience as they move through your business. Your marketing system must reliably and cost-effectively reach, engage, enroll, develop, and retain clients at scale. The two key outcomes of your marketing system are client relationships and earnings growth.

This notion of experience design (to earn profitable long-term relationships) speaks to the full scope of marketing. It also helps explain why it's so challenging to answer the "what is marketing?" question.

Marketing Is Not a Tactic

Hopefully, you're starting to see that marketing is not about describing your company or your products and services. It's not about websites or social media or any single tactic.

Marketing is the system you build to select and guide clients successfully through your business. When you put marketing in this context, you can relate everything you do in marketing to improving some segment of your customer's journey.

So, What Is Marketing?

Marketing is everything you do to grow your business. I like this definition because it's broad, inclusive, client-centric, and outcome-oriented.

Where to From Here?

This holistic view of marketing can seem too large to take on. It can seem intimidating, like "eating an elephant". It's why I wrote this book.

Don't let this expanded scope deter you. If you're willing to take small incremental steps towards a larger goal, you have a huge opportunity for growth. Once you start, you'll be amazed at how much progress you can make.

The 20 Ways of Being are meant to guide you on your path to marketing mastery.

DEFINING MASTERY

In the context of this book, I'm defining mastery or being masterful as having complete control over a practice area.

Customer-centric marketing is too diverse to enable one to gain personal mastery over its many facets. However, what you can do as a business owner, is become masterful at the application of marketing to achieve business objectives.

Try to imagine you're a symphony composer and a conductor with a large ensemble of marketing musicians. A competent orchestra can play anything, but there must first be a score to play, with a conductor to lead them.

As a business owner, if you can't justify hiring a chief marketing officer, the composer and conductor roles fall to you.

You must imagine the music and develop the score, assemble the musicians, practise and conduct them well.

Don't assume you need to know how to do everything yourself to lead your people. Remember you're the composer and conductor. You don't have to play all the instruments too.

Imagine a group of talented musicians (marketing folks) all doing their own thing, with no leadership or direction. You have a cacophony (noise or the opposite of music). A bunch of marketing activities with no leadership and direction performs just as poorly. You get random acts of marketing.

So What's Your Score (Your Plan)?

What are you designing, building, practising and mastering?

For many companies, there is no marketing plan. There's no one conducting their marketing activities. This lack of vision and coordination is why marketing often performs so poorly.

This book will help business owners with little to no marketing experience compose a score and conduct their marketing orchestra masterfully.

Just like anything that requires the development of mastery, you can't buy it. You must become it, with purpose, direction, coordination, and practise. It takes a lot of each of these inputs to become performance ready.

Think about marketing in the same way. It's not about buying advertising or building websites; it's about your company becoming an effective marketing machine which has practised and is performance ready.

Once you stop trying to buy marketing and start working to become it, you'll start making meaningful headway.

WHAT ARE WAYS OF BEING?

Ways of Being are rooted in the study of ontology and phenomenology.

Ways of Being refer to what's going on for you internally. It's your mental, emotional, and physical state in the moment. The Ways of Acting are your outward expression or your reactions to your inner Ways of Being. Your external expressions include your thoughts, your speaking, and what you're doing.

For simplicity's sake, I am collapsing the internal and external expressions into one and calling them Ways of Being or Ways for short.

I know this is an over-simplification, but I want to keep things as straightforward and actionable as possible.

If you'd like to learn about the principles behind Ways of Being and Acting, there are several resources available. Werner Erhard dedicated his career to the topic, and he has published many books and articles on the subject.

The study of mindfulness and cognitive behavioral therapy (CBT) are other theories to study to understand and gain mastery over the core mechanisms.

An introduction to the Ways of Being fundamentals will greatly aid you in the application of this book.

Enough Theory

Let's look at being kind as an example. There are hundreds of different behaviours you can use to express kindness.

No individual act of kindness constitutes being a kind person. However, a regular pattern of kind behaviours becomes a consistent and practised Way of Being.

We all have Ways of Being that people use to describe us. She is kind; he is honest; she is untrustworthy; he is inappropriate, etc. One incident does not a Way of Being create. It is the frequency and consistency of the behaviours that earn us our labels and results.

No one is a particular Way of Being all the time. We do, however, exhibit some Ways of Being with great regularity, and these patterns of behaviour are responsible for who people believe us to be.

Why Focus on Ways Of Being?

Your Ways of Being are largely responsible for the results you create for yourself in your life, your relationships, your career, and your business.

There are Ways of Being we're all familiar with and value, like being respectful, honest, trustworthy, resilient, collaborative, optimistic, generous, and resourceful.

However, you may not appreciate how much your Ways of Being are responsible for your goal achievements, your relationships, and pretty much everything.

The long-term cumulative effects of your Ways of Being shape and define your life. They also influence the lives of your family and your business.

Our collective Ways of Being define our culture, our institutions, and our governments. Suffice it to say that Ways of Being are far more important than we realise.

How Do You Choose Your Ways?

Consider that you use two broad patterns of decision-making in every moment. You choose your Way of Being either consciously or unconsciously based on how you choose to view a situation.

Conscious choosing comes from being thoughtful and deliberate in how you interpret a situation. It is where you make active decisions in alignment with your purpose, your goals and values, and who you want to be.

Unconscious choosing is when you're on autopilot. You default to a Way of Being rather than actively choosing it. In these situations, your unconscious ways may not align with your goals and values. You tend to make these unconscious choices when you're not paying attention, or you're fatigued, stressed, emotional, or distracted.

This book is about making the conscious choice to take on 20 specific Ways of Being to become who your clients need you to be.

This discussion about Ways of Being is a deliberate attempt to shift your business development efforts away from random acts of marketing (a focus on tools and tactics) to a customer-centric and systematic approach to marketing and business development.

Ways of Being includes things like who you choose as clients, your company culture, and your systems for goal achievement.

One of the key goals of this work is to accelerate the pace of relationship development and earnings growth.

To be clear, I'm not suggesting that marketing tools and tactics are bad. Who could argue their necessity? The problem I consistently experience is a focus on tactics out of context with any purpose, goals, process, or strategy.

The 20 Ways framework is the answer to the chaos and absence of leadership, planning, and accountability, rampant in marketing.

It boils down to practising and systematising the things that matter in a natural and logical sequence.

HOW THE WAYS WORK

The 20 Ways of Being are practices to own and implement over time as you design, build, and operate your business.

The Ways serve two purposes:

1. As a whole, they serve as a map, providing context for where you're going. They offer a holistic, behavioural, and systems view of business development.
2. Each Way is meant to be something to take on and master. Each new Way of Being builds upon the last. As you master each Way, you become more capable of succeeding in your business development efforts.

The 20 Ways are not strict, rigid, or mutually exclusive. You can, and in some cases will, benefit from working on several Ways at once. Just remember to consider the Ways in sequence and know that if you take on Way # 20 first, without laying the foundation built in the previous 19 Ways, your efforts will be inhibited by whatever Ways you skipped.

The Ways are grouped into three stages of business development: Design, Build, and Grow.

In the design stage, each Way defines your business more and more clearly. These Ways define your leadership platform (who you are, whom you serve, and what experience you are in business to create).

The Ways of Being in the build stage are about scaling your business.

The Ways in the grow stage focus on connecting with people and building relationships. They focus on recruiting, enrolling, and earning the loyalty of clients to maximise your earnings potential.

If you're a solo-practitioner or you operate a smaller scale business, the build stage will be less involved, but still important.

If you have a larger mature company, consider each Way in a diagnostic context. Determine whether the absence of a Way is inhibiting your success. Ask yourself if you need to revisit your systems, procedures, training, and coaching frameworks to bring about greater alignment, quality, and consistency of practice.

Don't be surprised if you find gaps and incongruencies in your existing systems. You may find you need to go back to the first few Ways to better define your goals and intentions before moving forward.

To see all the 20 Ways in context, please download the free Ways of Being poster at Accruemarketing.com/20WaysMap.

It's useful to visualise all 20 Ways of Being at the same time, the way you would view a map. This map is what I started looking for from day one in business, and I'm excited to provide you with what I was so desperate to find.

I admit; if I were presented with this map back then, I would not have known how to read it. I would have needed this book to explain how to navigate and implement Ways of Being.

There Is No Correct Way to Practise

As you are learning about each Way of Being, you might find it frustrating that I'm not giving you a specific task or action to take.

This is intentional because there are no specific or universal patterns to follow. How you practise a Way will depend on your needs, and those of your company as well as the needs of your clients.

What is important is the intention or the purpose behind each Way.

For each Way, you need to ask yourself, "How are we going to develop, adopt, practise, systematise, measure and refine this Way in our business?"

Each Way represents a leadership opportunity for you to grow into.

Each Way is also a litmus test for new ideas and technologies. When confronted with "the next best thing", ask yourself which Way(s) of Being does this idea or gizmo fit into? How will we incorporate it into our system, to improve our practice and our results?

Simply asking these questions will guard against the dreaded random acts of marketing.

Suggestions for How to Use This Book

Start by downloading the 20 Ways of Being Poster at AccrueMarketing.com/20WaysMap. Look at the Ways in their entirety as you would plan a trip with a road map.

The Ways are more or less linear and you should be able to recognise where you are on the map. You can see which Ways you are practising now, and which ones you skipped over or are struggling with.

Then focus on the gaps. The highest leverage gaps will be the Ways closest to the beginning since every Way builds on the ones that came before.

Often, you'll find the reason your marketing is not working well is because you skipped a Way or two earlier in the process.

Skimmers

If you want to skim the book, I suggest reading the first three sections of each chapter to get the gist of the idea. This will give you the introduction, the why, and the cost of not practising a specific Way.

When you are ready to take on a Way, go back and re-read the entire chapter. Consider starting from the beginning and taking on one or two chapters at a time.

Alternatively, look for a chapter you think represents your biggest opportunity and dig in.

The Structure of Each Chapter

Each chapter introduces one Way of Being, it outlines why a Way is important, and discusses the implications of not practising the Way.

Instruction is offered on how to practise a Way. Each chapter asks you a series of questions to help get you started and then provides key resources to direct your learning, development, and mastery.

PATTERNS OF USE

While the 20 Ways are intended to be universal, you can approach them differently depending on the type of company you operate and your stage of development.

Franchisees

As franchisees, you have attached yourself to a pre-existing brand, infrastructure, and promotional framework. The Ways that apply most to you include:

> Being responsive
>
> Being informed
>
> Being accessible
>
> Being connected
>
> Being endorsable
>
> Being present
>
> Being conspicuous

Corporate Professionals

Much like a franchisee, corporate professionals are supposed to embody the corporate brand and follow the company program.

However, you still need to apply the 20 Ways to your individual practice development, your professional network, and your client/account development.

You have a great deal of latitude in how you practise. As such, nearly all the Ways still apply to you personally.

Start-ups

The Ways were designed specifically for start-ups. The sequence of Ways is relevant for you as presented.

Growth Enterprises

For growth enterprises, the Ways are more likely to be used as either a diagnostic tool or an approach to achieve breakthrough results.

To use the Ways as a diagnostic tool, start by reviewing how you are living into each way.

Start with being intentional and assess whether your mission is still fuzzy or perhaps out of date. Then look at each Way critically, relative to that core intention.

Next look closely at being systematic, being informed, and being effective. These are common gaps and problem areas.

Look closely at each of the five Ways in the grow stage to determine their effectiveness. If they are not performing well, backtrack to being relevant, affective, attractive, and compelling as potential problem areas.

If there is still no smoking gun, look at each Way independently, and you'll uncover the gaps inhibiting your growth and profitability.

For breakthrough results, be willing to rethink how you approach marketing. What would it look like if you lived into all 20 Ways?

A WARNING

The Ways of Being are not a quick fix. They are not something you can implement in three months or even a year. The Ways are practices to learn and integrate into your habits, culture, systems, and processes.

As a solopreneur, you might see the Ways as a three to five-year plan. Well-financed, growth-driven companies might be able to grow into these Ways within 18 months, if you have great leadership, and the resources to finance the program.

A large mature company could take the longest to adopt the Ways, despite its resources. Why? Because the Ways may present as the opposite of what you are doing now.

You have inertia and investment in what you've been doing, and you're unlikely to shift direction without pain and resistance. Fortunately, if you can lead people through the transformation, you'll be best equipped to invest in the process and reap the rewards.

Some of the most troubling client stories I've seen are from the mature companies with no marketing program to speak of. They've spent, in some cases, a hundred years, spending their considerable annual budgets on this and that, without ever laying tracks. Each year they start over with a large budget for a new batch of busywork.

Despite their age, they never outgrew their random acts of marketing approach. Imagine what they would have accomplished with a plan they worked at a little at a time over 20+ years.

Introduction

The Ways of Being might seem intimidating at first but don't worry, they are not as daunting as they might seem.

They require no more effort and time than learning to play a musical instrument well or becoming a black belt in karate.

You will not master the Ways in three months, but you can make a great deal of progress very quickly if you choose to.

It's like learning to play your first few basic songs well on the piano. After three months, you won't sound anything like the prodigies with years of practise, but you will be playing music.

The Ways are best developed over time with patience, dedication, training, and practise—just like everything else you choose to learn and master.

In my consulting practice, I find the main things people struggle with are impatience, and resistance to change. To overcome this, I encourage them to think "small daily practices, accrue big results over time".

I like to visualise ocean waves relentlessly pounding at cliffs, and the steady march of erosion, to get my head into the practises.

You are the ever-persistent waves and not the resistant cliff in this analogy.

THE
DESIGN STAGE

Developing Your Leadership Platform

THE DESIGN STAGE

The first nine Ways are strategic facets of what we call your leadership platform. They are also the foundation of your sales and marketing program.

These Ways include:

Being intentional – defining your purpose

Being committed – investing in a course of action

Being competitive – owning your positioning

Being recognisable – presenting consistently

Being relevant – occurring as an opportunity

Being affective – connecting emotionally

Being attractive – expressing authentically

Being compelling – creating urgency

Being knowable – achieving transparency

Your leadership platform is who you are committed to being as an individual leader and as a company. You use your leadership platform to communicate the many facets of your intentions, which serve to guide your collective actions.

Your leadership platform is the essence or core of your brand, your story, and your key sales messaging.

Your platform helps you enroll people in your vision, and it informs the experience you want people to have of you.

In a customer-centric framework, you're not pitching what you do or how great you are. You're helping clients realise how what you're offering will help them meet a need or achieve an objective.

Customer-centric implies guiding clients through their decision making and purchase process, from their point of view.

This approach is essential in all kinds of relationship-based businesses, particularly in professional services. It is important anywhere an ongoing relationship is desired.

The challenge for most of us is learning to think like our clients and to communicate with them on their terms.

INTENTIONAL

Defining Your Purpose

"Clarity affords focus."

Thomas Lenard

THE DESIGN STAGE

BEING INTENTIONAL

About Being Intentional

Being intentional is about getting clear and specific about what your company is and does, whom you serve, your reasons for being, and more.

Many of us think we are clear in our intention because we spend so much time thinking about and engaged in our businesses.

However, if you have not yet documented your business concept in a precise and structured way, you're likely not as clear in your intention as you think you are.

Being intentional is about developing a comprehensive and unified description of your business to help you and your team get on the same page. It's an exercise in purpose, clarity, specificity, and alignment.

Think of your company as a wheel and yourself as the axel the wheel revolves around. A lack of intention (like a bent axel) creates an annoying and destructive vibration and wobble that increases in intensity as you accelerate (grow your company).

Clarifying your intention eliminates the wobble from who you are being as a leader, allowing everyone to get behind you, and for your company to accelerate smoothly.

Why Is Being Intentional Necessary?

Your purpose as a leader is to set direction; to reach, engage, and enroll people in your company's purpose. The more focused your intention as a leader, the more likely you are to inspire (staff, investors, clients, your peers, the media, etc.) and bring them on board with your mission.

The four reasons to be intentional.

1. You need to know where you're going so you don't confuse everyone around you or allow yourself to be swayed by distractions and people trying to make you veer off in new directions.

2. Your ability to clearly, consistently, and confidently articulate your intentions, enables other people to understand you and decide whether they agree with you. Your clarity of intention helps them decide whether they want to support you in some capacity.

3. As soon as you declare your intentions, you take a stand for or against. You begin to attract like-minded people while repelling those with opposing positions.

4. Once your intentions are clear, it makes it easier for others to provide meaningful referrals.

The Costs of Not Being Intentional

If you're not sure where you're going, how can anyone truly follow you?

Think of being intentional as the foundation that everything else you do is built upon. The more you delay getting clear and being intentional, the greater the risk that everything completed beforehand will need to be revisited.

There are three practical costs of lacking clear intention. They are time, money, and effort.

Simply stated, it's harder, more time consuming, and costly to achieve almost anything when you are unclear in your intentions.

In the book *The Seven Habits of Highly Effective People*, Stephen Covey calls it "starting with the end in mind". If there is one Way of Being that powerfully contributes to your success, it is your clarity of intention.

How to Practise Being Intentional

You need to work at two levels: 1. yourself personally and 2. your business.

Why are you taking this mission on? What are you hoping to achieve? Ask the same questions about your business.

In classic terms, you become more intentional by getting clear on your mission, vision, and values.

You get clear on what you and your company do; who you are in service of; what your unique selling proposition is; and how you plan to sustain a competitive advantage.

"Once you clarify your mission, you can live into that intention."

Living into your intention is about the consistency of words and actions. It's about creating alignment by eliminating things which are out of alignment. People, processes, practices, and products all need to line up.

Once you're clear, consistent, and acting in alignment with your intentions, there is a sort of harmony that occurs. People call it the law of attraction.

Being intentional is attractive, and it draws like to like. It's difficult to describe. It triggers a constructive coalescence, like wave harmonics.

The Call to Action

It doesn't matter what stage of business you're in; consider your clarity of intention. How clear and deliberate are you? Where are the opportunities to further clarify your intentions and create greater internal alignment between your intentions and your actions?

Don't be fooled into thinking you've done this work already because you've been through a mission, vision, and values exercise. In my experience, many of these efforts lack specificity. They are too superficial and lack a sense of purpose.

If you want to test your intentionality, ask your people if they're clear on your intentions. Have them point out where you fall short. Their answers will be telling.

Most likely, you'll need to refine your intentions to a level you're unfamiliar with. You start by mapping out each facet of your business idea. Then be as specific as you can be with your answers.

Choose your words carefully as the power of intention begins with how clearly you articulate your purpose. The way you describe what you're up to needs to be consistent and inspiring.

Please don't rush through the process or diminish its importance. This work is the foundation of your company.

Thoughts and Action Planning

Start by answering these questions as specifically as you can.

1. What is the core purpose of your business?

2. Who are you in business to serve? Specifically.

3. What is your core innovation as a company? What problem do you solve for people? Or what opportunity do you represent?

4. Why would a prospective client choose you over your competition?

5. Why would anyone follow your leadership or invest in your business?

If you can't answer these questions clearly, get some help. You need to be intentional before you have any hope of being committed.

Resources for Being Intentional

The first and most valuable resource for getting clear on your intentions is a marketing coach, business coach, or strategy consultant.

They'll push you to refine your thinking further and further until all the pieces fit nicely together into a documented set of values, a mission, a vision, and a strategic plan of action.

Normally, I'm a firm believer in do-it-yourself efforts, but in this case, do yourself a favour and get some help. You'll shave years off your developmental timeline and save thousands on ill-fated efforts.

As a starting point, visit the Free Stuff page on our website for the list of free eBooks. AccrueMarketing.com/free-marketing-downloads/

The First Seven Questions eBook is relevant to this chapter.

We also offer a six-module program called Creating Clarity, designed specifically to help small business owners through this work.

For something more substantial, read:

Start With Why:
How Great Leaders Inspire Everyone To Take Action
Simon Sinek

——— BEING ———
COMMITTED

Invested in a Course Of Action

"It's hard to beat a person who never gives up."

Babe Ruth

THE DESIGN STAGE

BEING COMMITTED

About Being Committed

There are two kinds of commitments. The first are ones you make without thinking, then begrudgingly live with. Getting a tattoo while under the influence or purchasing an expensive timeshare while on vacation are examples of this. You're committed in that you're stuck with it, but not in a good way.

Then there are commitments you make with a clear head and due consideration. You plan, research, get advice, weigh options relative to goals and costs, then you commit with intention. "You are in it, to win it" so to speak.

You can commit to a business either way. However, in this conversation, we're talking about the clear-headed, rational, well-considered, "I know full well what I am getting myself into" kind of commitments. You know what you're doing, and you're committed to making it happen because it's an opportunity worthy of you.

Where are you with your business? Do you regret starting it? Are you making the best of a bad decision, or are you excited and doggedly determined to succeed?

Why Is Being Committed Necessary?

Rarely does anything great come into being without a "do or die" kind of commitment. Without it, you complain, you make excuses, you hedge, procrastinate, and generally find reasons not to succeed. Without commitment, you are easily stopped.

People have compared being in business to a very long distance, off-road triathlon, only longer and more gruelling. Real commitment is essential, or you won't stick it out long enough to succeed.

The Costs of Not Being Committed

A lack of commitment costs you nothing short of your dreams. It leaves you wondering what might have been. It leaves you frustrated and powerless.

What does your lack of commitment cost you: success, fulfillment, happiness? Commitment represents the life you want for yourself.

The costs of not committing are extremely high. What's it going to take for you to step into a do or die commitment with your life and business?

How to Practise Being Committed

Just as there are two types of commitment, there are two broad stages as well. The first stage is about making a big decision. The second is learning how to live into and to escalate your commitment when everyone and everything is challenging you to stop.

Let's focus on the first type of commitment—deciding to commit.

Making the Decision

If you're clear on your intentions but not yet committed, you tend to move along with your initiative until you run into something that exceeds the limits of your discretionary spending. This is a crucial point where you will either stop, or you will find a way.

You must decide:

1. Do I stop because I'm not that committed?
2. Do I step up my commitment and invest?
3. Do I find third party investors and keep going?
4. Do I scale back, and alter my plans to stay inside my financial comfort zone?

The same thing happens with your time. You have discretionary time to invest as well. As soon as your initiative begins to infringe too much on your work, personal routines, friends and family, you need to commit or alter your plans.

Your capacity to handle complexity, learn quickly, communicate, delegate, self-manage, and deal with stress will all challenge your resolve and require you to deepen your commitment.

The most demanding factors are often your friends and family who don't understand, who disagree with your choices, and want you to stop taking unnecessary risks and to do what they want you to do. Take the so-called safe route.

Big commitments challenge you to step up and learn how to deal with unknowns. You need to decide whether you're prepared to step up and be who you need to be and do what you need to do, to realise your goals.

If that sounds like a lot to deal with, it can be, and it often is.

How do you decide if you're all-in, ready to scale-back, or if it's time to cut and run? I'm afraid there are no easy answers. The answers come down to a mix of factors that include: your reasons, the business opportunity, your relationships, your willingness to learn, and to seek and accept help.

I urge you to consider the following list of questions carefully as they all have the potential to derail your efforts and make you reconsider your commitment to your business.

Your Personal Reasons

Why do you want to start or operate this business? Do you know? It's an important question that warrants an answer. Are you looking for freedom? Are you seeking fame and fortune? Are you trying to solve a problem? Are you trying to live your passion? Are you trying to prove something to yourself or someone else? Are you trying to earn a living and put money away for retirement?

Do you know your why? It's challenging to commit to something when you're not clear why you're doing it.

The Business Opportunity

Is the business idea viable and worth committing to? Can you make any money at it? Is there any demand for the business? Is the business

41

scalable? Can you maintain a competitive advantage over time? Have you developed a budget and cash flow model to estimate cash flow requirements and your return on investment? Is this an investment you expect to get a competitive return on, or is it a labour of love? Have you considered the risk factors and how you plan to mitigate your risks?

Your Relationships

Have you considered the implications of your business on your relationships? What does your spouse or partner think of it? Are they onboard and fully behind you, or are they tolerating or opposed to your business? Are you going to be able to move your business forward, or will your partner roadblock you as soon as you need to invest beyond your discretionary income?

Will you be able to juggle your personal and family commitments?

There are no right answers, but it's important to take the time to think about these questions and discuss them with your family before you leap into your venture.

Although it may sound strange, consider a written agreement with your partner detailing what you are both agreeing to in advance. Have the conversations necessary to formalise what commitments you are making. Make sure to discuss your risk tolerance, anticipated levels of investment, how you plan to make decisions, timeframes involved, and what the end game is.

Your Willingness to Learn

Going into business is a learning opportunity, as long as you're willing to see it that way.

You'll need to actively take on dozens of learning curves on topics you have no interest in, on an ongoing basis. If you don't like to learn, hate to read, don't like getting feedback or learning from others, you may wish to reconsider your decision to own a business.

The continuous learning demands may challenge your resolve.

Your Resistance to Planning

Making commitments and living into them is challenging at the best of times. Succeeding in business will likely be the biggest and most challenging commitment of your life, next to parenting.

If you're not prepared to put in the effort answering some basic questions now, ask yourself if you'll put in the effort and expense to succeed.

The Call to Action

Don't wait until you encounter a big obstacle before you decide if you're committed. The sooner you understand your true goals and your level of commitment, the more time, money, and effort you'll save for the things you're committed to.

You know yourself and how you make decisions. Ask yourself if you have the self-discipline to make a rational decision or if you need to engage a mentor, a coach, or a trusted advisor to help you decide.

Thoughts and Action Planning

1. What is your Why?

2. How will this business serve you?

3. What are the biggest risks and obstacles you expect to deal with?

4. Why is your business plan worthy of investment?

5. Is your partner on board?

6. Are you willing to learn, and to seek out and take the advice of others?

7. How will you finance your plan and manage the cash flow requirements?

8. How long are you willing to struggle to make your business work?

9. What's your exit plan?

10. What will it take to get you to fully commit to your plan?

Resources for Being Committed

To help you commit, the core elements of a plan include:

- a competitive review
- a specific target customer
- an assessment of demand
- a risk assessment
- sales targets and performance constraints
- promotional and sales plans
- a staffing plan
- a budget and forecast model

Resist the urge to think this is overkill. It's not as painful as it looks.

Remember, you are doing this analysis for yourself, not the bank. It's to help you understand what you're getting into before you start.

It's much safer to invest the time in planning than it is to invest real money without understanding costs, risks, and expected returns.

The challenge for many when building their plan is forecasting results and learning how to convert advertising and sales expenses to revenue and earnings. The expense and conversion assumptions need to come from somewhere.

The main resources you'll need are inputs from a marketing strategist, a business analyst, and your accountant. The rest you can accomplish with a spreadsheet and a healthy dose of patience.

—— BEING ——
COMPETITIVE

Owning Your Positioning

"Any master of his craft knows that it is not his opponent he is fighting. It is himself."

Chae Richardson

THE DESIGN STAGE

BEING COMPETITIVE

About Being Competitive

Being competitive is something we're all familiar with on a personal level. We feel it in ourselves. We see it in our friends and family members. Our pets compete and even our garden plants compete for light.

But what does being competitive mean? It doesn't mean we need to be the best in the world or even the best in the city. In this conversation, we're defining being competitive as choosing and living into a set of competitive factors valued and preferred by your target audience.

It means making a conscious choice about what your business will compete on.

Thankfully, there are dozens of factors to choose from.

Common competitive options include price, ease or simplicity, convenience, speed, design, capability, compatibility, expertise, experience, service, reliability, quality, versatility, prestige, and more.

The question is, which competitive factors are you building your business around? How do you intend to exploit and expand upon your competitive distinction?

Why Is Being Competitive Necessary?

The simple answer to why compete is because the factors you choose enable you to differentiate yourself and your offerings from your competitors. Your choices allow you to align with what matters most to you and your target audience.

There's little point in being the low-price leader in a luxury marketplace, for example.

Choosing your audience and what you plan to compete on defines who you become. It defines your competitors too. Once you name your competitors, you can determine where the bar is set and what you need to do to be competitive or to lead the category.

Your competitive strategy determines how difficult you make it for others to compete with you.

How sustainable is your competitive advantage? Is there anything about your advantage that will be difficult for others to replicate in short order? Is there anything you can do to step out of the box and do something completely contrary to industry norms and practices? If you can, and your target clients deem it valuable, you might have found your competitive edge.

The Costs of Not Being Competitive

The costs of not being competitive, in the simplest terms, are lost sales and lower profit margins. In the absence of a competitive strategy, the market defaults to price, which is a difficult position to own.

Your competitive strategy defines your focus, direction, innovation schedule, operating practices, price, and margin. Without clarity on your competitive strategy, you effectively choose to make it harder for people to understand why they should select you.

By not actively choosing your competitive strategy, you lose a vital sense of purpose and direction.

You also lose the benefit of speaking directly to your target audience about what matters most to them and how you are the obvious choice.

If you don't tell them why, they'll need to figure it out on their own, and chances are they won't bother. If you can't figure it out, why would anyone else do it for you?

How to Practise Being Competitive

The practice of being competitive begins with being honest with yourself about what's important to you, and your ability to deliver on it.

You may wish to be a luxury brand, but if you're the low price provider, you're better off running with it, rather than pretending to be something you're not.

You must be authentic about your competitive positioning, or people will reject your offering, and bad mouth you for good measure.

You need to understand your target audience. What are their needs, what motivates them, what is their research and decision process? What do they buy now? What do they hate about the current options? What do they want desperately to find in a competitive offer? In short, you need to get to know your clients.

You also need to get to know your competitors. What do they do? What do they charge? How long do they take to deliver? What service do they provide? What do people love and hate about them? What is the chink in their armour? Where is your opportunity to shine relative to them?

You need to know where you sit relative to the leaders, the pack and the stragglers. You need to be clear what competitive game you're playing, and then you need to play it.

Just like in sports, living into a competitive strategy takes time and commitment. You can't oscillate from one competitive strategy to the next. You must own yours and live into it fully.

You also need objective feedback and direction. It's difficult to stay objective about your performance without insightful feedback from a coach, your clients, and subject matter experts.

Who will you invite into your camp to help you compete?

The Call to Action

If you haven't completed a competitive review or analysis yet, do it now. Few tasks pay greater dividends than getting a clear sense of the market and where you fit into it.

A competitive analysis can offer you a much-needed dose of reality.

Start simple with a SWOT (strengths, weaknesses, opportunities, threats) analysis. Then expand this effort into a list of local, regional, and national competitors who are visible online and within your community.

Look closely at your competitors' offerings, decode their positioning and determine who they're selling to. Think about your target audience and the factors they use to make purchase decisions. Where do your competitors rank on each decision factor (speed, price, quality, etc.)?

Use a spreadsheet to help you see the patterns and identify gaps. Look at their websites, social media profiles, online reviews, and investor information (if they're a public company). There is often a lot of readily-available information to help you decode a competitor's strategy without too much effort and expense.

You don't need a perfect understanding to get the lay-of-the-land. You only need enough information to see where you fit into the competitive landscape.

If you don't have time, hire a consultant to help you. Don't wait too long to get it done or you'll end up wasting time and effort backtracking.

Thoughts and Action Planning

1. Who are you competing with, in your trade area?

2. Who are you competing with online?

3. What alternative offerings are you competing with from your indirect competitors?

4. Which factors are your competitors focused on?

5. Which factor(s) are you choosing to compete on?

6. How are your top competitors marketing and driving sales?

7. What's your plan to compete with them?

Resources for Being Competitive

The two books I generally recommend as a starting point are:

Competitive Strategy

Techniques for Analyzing Industries and Competitors
by Michael E. Porter

Blue Ocean Strategy

How to Create Uncontested Market Space and Make the Competition Irrelevant
by W. Chan Kim & Renee Mauborgne

Internet marketing is the other area to look into

Look at your website and your competitors' websites with:

Alexa.com

Look at their Alexa score, their backlink count, and where their traffic is coming from compared to yours.

Website.grader.com

Use this free tool to get feedback on your website and where you need to pull up your socks.

Nibler.com

Nibler offers a comprehensive site and marketing grader that is worth a look as well.

—— BEING ——
RECOGNISABLE

Presenting Consistently

"Create your own visual style ... let it be unique for yourself and yet identifiable for others."

Orson Welles

THE DESIGN STAGE

BEING RECOGNISABLE

About Being Recognisable

Being recognisable is about creating a workable identity and then applying it consistently. People often think of their identity as their name and logo. However, for an identity to hold up to actual use, you need a far more extensive kit.

Besides your name, domain name, wordmark, and logo, you will need a square aspect ratio icon for social media (that works from 600x600 pixels down to a 16x16 pixel favicon). You will want a positioning line, a short introduction, a functional colour palette, and a variety of textures for visual interest. You should also include a set of fonts (typefaces) that can be used easily in print, online, and embroidery.

Your photography is also critical. You need so-called hero shots of yourself and your products, as well as images that represent your clients and your location if you serve customers there. The photos should reflect your colours, style, and quality standards.

If you plan to advertise extensively, consider whether you need a slogan, a jingle, or sonic branding to round out your kit.

There are other non-visual or perceptual factors to include in your identity—things like your sense of style, your energy level or vibe. Subtle experience factors can all be elements that make you instantly recognisable.

Your kit will be unique to you and how your business operates. What's important is to apply your identity consistently, as it has an important job to do. It needs to help people recognise you and pigeonhole you quickly and accurately.

Why Is Being Recognisable Necessary?

You become recognisable via the consistent use of your identity. Unless you're the face of your business, your company needs a face of its own that it can wear without alteration for years.

Think of your identity kit as how people recognise you in any situation, (in-person, in print, and online).

You want your identity to convey a constructive meaning, so it becomes synonymous with your value proposition.

Bear in mind how quickly people recognise and judge everything. It's important to create an identity that represents you well.

The Costs of Not Being Recognisable

If people do not recognise you, there is no cumulative effect from repeated exposure. Without being recognisable, you don't build up social equity, meaning, or value in the marketplace.

If you don't present a thoughtful and consistent look, people will judge your lack of attention as a reflection of how you do business; reinforcing a negative perception of you and your company.

For something that seems so subtle and insignificant, it is surprisingly important, so ignore it at your peril.

How to Practise Being Recognisable

The practice of being recognisable involves making sure you show up consistently in any context without deviating from your identity standards.

You apply your identity standard to everything your clients and prospects have contact with.

The easiest place to start is with your email footer, stationery, business cards, social media profiles, and directory listings, invoices, cheques, and envelopes, as these are regular use items.

Depending on your business, name badges, uniforms, decor items, signage, vehicle wraps, and even accent clothing should be considered.

Other important factors include your website, your physical place of business, or your retail space. These environments are the most complex as your identity has so many forms of expression.

Advertising and promotional items are next. They too build upon your identity standards.

The Call to Action

Don't make the mistake of thinking you can put off creating a functional identity kit. It is much more important than people realise. It's very costly to redo everything with a new identity after the fact, considering your name, domain, logo, and colours are on everything.

I see so many start-up companies ignoring their identities or selling the process short. What they show their clients is they don't place much value on their image or their communication materials.

Within weeks, they realise they've spent a lot of money on business essentials that all need to be redone. They realise their identity is non-functional, incomplete, and does not represent who they are or whom they serve.

Their visual identity becomes unworkable in short order and an impediment to growth. What starts out as a cost-saving effort, ends up being a very costly mistake.

Do yourself a favour and invest in an identity kit. Work with a strategist and a designer. Make sure your designer has both print and online experience. I still see identities developed that ignore online requirements and end up needing to be revised or redone to compensate.

You need to understand the importance and functional requirements of your visual identity. Don't assume your designer will anticipate the full scope of your needs.

Include a marketing strategist on your team as he will help you and your designer understand your requirements, how to prioritise your needs, and how to budget appropriately.

You don't need to spend a fortune on your identity. You can keep it very simple and have it look great and work well. What's important is that you understand the expectations of your market. You want to look a cut above your competitors, but not over the top for your industry, as that will look bad too.

You don't need to start with the whole kit either. You do, however, need a plan, so you don't look uncoordinated as you piece your kit together.

Identity is one of the areas we recommend you seek help with. It is very difficult to develop an identity as a do-it-yourself project.

Thoughts and Action Planning

Answer these questions to gain a sense of where you are now with Being Recognisable.

1. Have you created a document that defines your brand, identity, and voice?

2. Do you use a meaningful positioning line or tagline to help clarify what you do?

3. Do you have a functional logo and a social media icon?

4. Do you have a functional colour palette you use consistently in print and on the web?

5. Do you have professional photography of you, your location, and your products?

6. What fonts or typefaces do you use consistently?

7. What is the voice of your company from the standpoint of tone, attitude, energy, friendliness, and formality?

Resources for Being Recognisable

To help you understand what's involved in building your brand and identity, a Free eBook called *Branding and Identity* is available at AccrueMarketing.com. Please visit the **Free Stuff** page.

Books that cover the topic well include:

Designing Brand Identity
An Essential Guide for the Whole Branding Team
by Alina Wheeler

How to Style Your Brand:
Everything You Need to Know to Create a Distinctive Brand Identity
by Fiona Humberstone

—— BEING ——
RELEVANT

Occurring As An Opportunity

*"Make your marketing so useful
people would pay for it."*

Jack Baer

THE DESIGN STAGE

BEING RELEVANT

About Being Relevant

There are many ways to be relevant. You can be admired, desired, beautiful, topical, stylish, influential, useful, entertaining, thought-provoking, or innovative, to name a few.

What's important is you don't decide what is relevant; your clients decide as do their surrogates, the search engines.

To be relevant to anyone besides yourself, you need to first choose who you're seeking to be relevant to, and to speak to them directly.

Ideally, you speak to people about who they are, what they find important, what they're struggling with or hoping to achieve. How will they suffer in the absence of a solution? What will they gain if they get what they want?

Yes, you and your products are important, but you need to put what you do into the context of your clients' needs if you want them to care.

Remember "What's in it for me?" is the golden rule in marketing.

You become relevant by choosing an audience and speaking to their needs and goals in a manner they find interesting, inspiring, entertaining, or useful. The same goes for search engines, but they determine your relevance in different ways.

Why Is Being Relevant Necessary?

If you're going to spend time and money promoting your business with advertising or any form of promotion, you had better be relevant, because the alternative is to be viewed as irrelevant or worse yet, invisible. You need to connect with people and help them appreciate you as an opportunity.

Relevance is particularly important on the internet due to the distracted and hurried usage patterns. People are too distracted to pay attention to anything that is not highly relevant to them. You need to be relevant, or you get lost, ignored, or discarded.

The Costs of Not Being Relevant

The short answer to why being relevant is important is poor sales and marketing performance, elongated sales cycle times, wasted money, lost opportunity and low regard by clients, peers, and potential employees. Low relevance increases cost and effort at every turn, and the effects are cumulative.

The more times you become irrelevant, the more ingrained the sentiment amongst your clients. Suffice it to say; irrelevance can be very costly.

How to Practise Being Relevant

Being relevant is about connecting with your clients in a way they relate to and find useful.

Define Your Target Audience

To be relevant, you start with who you want to be relevant to. Be as specific as possible. Divide your audiences up into the specific roles people play and the reasons for their purchases. Categorise and name each group. Think of who you could reach out to for an insider's perspective. Who would be a great representatives for each target audience?

Conduct Information Interviews

Consider selecting representatives of each target audience and set up interviews to discuss their situation, needs, purchase decision process, and the factors that most influence their decision making.

Ask for their perceptions on what they like and would like to see from providers. Your goal is to create a set of client personas.

Developing Client Personas

Client personas are fictitious profiles of people (amalgams of several real people) meant to represent your target buyers. Personas define who your marketing and sales communication must be relevant to.

You prepare one persona for each buyer type. Generally, they include an introduction, a demographic profile, information about their situation, what's important to them, target objectives, and how to support their purchase decision making.

The point of creating personas is to help you communicate directly with that specific person, in a way they'll connect with.

Uncover Trigger Events

Purchases tend to result from trigger events of some sort. When trigger events occur, a chain of predictable purchases follow. Think of moving into a new house, having a baby, or sending a child off to school as common triggers that stimulate predictable spending patterns.

What are the events that trigger your clients to start researching and buying from you?

Trigger events are prime opportunities to anticipate client needs and prepare highly relevant and timely communication.

Define Your Keyword Targets

When prospective clients seek out help online, they've been conditioned to visit search engines as one of their first steps. Because they don't yet know you, they will likely start with categorical searches for potential providers. What keywords are they likely to use? Do you know?

Search engines record search data and make it available to you. One way to be relevant is to align your messaging with how people seek help. Being relevant is what keyword research is all about.

Develop Use Cases

A use case is a sequential description of your client's research and decision process.

If you know what people need to make a decision, you can prepare it in advance for them.

Giving people what they need, when they need it, is a great way to make your content relevant and valuable.

Consider Customer-Centric Marketing

The process just described places the client at the centre of the sales and marketing process. Being customer-centric is the opposite of product-centric marketing.

Client-centric communication is about speaking to a client's needs rather than pitching a specific offering. Hopefully, you can see which approach is best for your business.

It's important to note, being customer-centric does not replace product-centric communication. It just moves your product information back a step or two, as you first engage your customer with what's important to them.

Learn Solution Selling and Active Communication

If you sell through a sales team, you'll want to select a solution-focused sales model with a communication style to match.

You can choose to facilitate a client's decision process, or you can choose to pitch them on your agenda.

There is no correct approach, only the one that fits your business model.

Learning to engage your clients with active listening and solution-focused communication is often perceived as more relevant and valuable by the client. The result is often an increase in trust and shorter sales cycle times.

The Call to Action

Stop fixating on your product. Get into your clients' heads and start communicating with them about their needs and objectives.

It sounds easy but learning to think and communicate from another's perspective can be unfamiliar. It takes time to learn how to take on the perspective of, and empathise with, your target audience.

Frankly, it takes a lot of time and effort. It's an area where engaging a marketing firm to guide you, will save time and effort.

Regardless of how you do it, get to know your clients, understand their needs, their triggers, and how they search and make decisions. The more relevant you can be, the more naturally sales will occur.

Thoughts and Action Planning

The key to being relevant is to write as though you were speaking to a specific person. Your target persona. Get into who they are and how they think.

1. Who are your target personas?

2. Write a one or two paragraph description about each persona. Start with bullets. Focus on their responsibilities and relevant demographics.

3. What trigger events regularly precede a purchase?

4. What's motivating their purchase?

5. What's their decision process?

6. What information will they need to make a purchase decision?

7. How will they describe your solution? What might they type into a search engine?

Resources for Being Relevant

The best books I'm aware of include:

SPIN Selling
by Neil Rackham
The book has been around a long time and is well regarded.

I've been a fan of this methodology for 20+ years. Despite the focus on direct selling, it's highly relevant to marketing and the creation of buyer personas and empathy maps.

Other resources to look into are:

Buyer Personas
How to Gain Insight into Your Customer's Expectations. Align Your Marketing Strategies and Win More Business
by Adele Revella

The Essential Persona Lifecycle:
Your Guide to Building and Using Personas
by Tamara Adlin and John Pruitt

Shift
Harness The Trigger Events That Turn Prospects into Customers
by Craig Elias and Tibor Shanto

—— BEING ——
AFFECTIVE

Connecting Emotionally

"The desire to reach for the stars is ambitious.
The desire to reach hearts is wise."

Maya Angelou

THE DESIGN STAGE

BEING AFFECTIVE

About Being Affective

Being affective is about connecting with people at an emotional level.

Some of us are more rational and dispassionate than others, but we are all emotional beings. We may not like it, but our emotions tend to govern our purchase behaviours more than we want to admit.

Each of us has different emotional priorities and traits; some with long-term orientations, while others are more impulse-based. Purchases tend to serve both emotional and practical needs.

Some of the most common emotions underlying purchase behaviours relate in some way to our unconscious fears, while others serve our desire to look good.

Your clients might be stressed, unhappy, or highly motivated to bring about change or to achieve a goal as quickly as possible.

Trust and confidence are two of the most important factors in sales, and you need to determine how to elicit both.

There are always values and beliefs in play that you need to connect with; such as environmental, social, national, religious, political, and ethical agendas as well as technical affiliations.

To sell and market effectively, you need to understand the emotional context behind why people buy, and where you and your company stand on important issues.

You want to make authentic emotional connections with your clients; which makes you more relatable, desirable, likeable, praiseworthy, and trustworthy.

Why Is Being Affective Necessary?

Even if you're selling heavy equipment to engineers, emotion is still part of the equation. We can't escape emotional decision-making.

If you're focused on facts and data, emotion is still being served. Something like "confidence and fear of making the wrong decision" would be a likely guess.

The bottom line is, if you understand and have empathy for your clients' emotional motivations, you can speak to them in your marketing.

If you connect at an emotional level, you become more relevant, desirable, sharable, and you're likely to be more profitable.

The Costs of Not Being Affective

You can use emotions to your advantage, or you can ignore them at your peril.

The cost of not focusing on emotions comes down to time and money. If you don't connect with people emotionally, you are deemed less relevant by clients, and the result is higher costs, slower sales, and less profit.

How to Practise Being Affective

You start being affective by getting to know and understand your clients' motivations. What are they trying to avoid or attain with their purchase? Try to look past the obvious and get into what's really behind their motivation to buy.

A new suit can be about a job. A big powerful 4x4 can be about bigger hauls or getting deeper into the woods. A sports car can represent status, fun, freedom, sex appeal, or fear of death.

Stereotypes might be a fun place to start, but that's not what being affective is about. You're trying to speak to people in a way that resonates with their inner, often undisclosed or unconscious, motivations.

One of the easiest ways to practise being affective is by asking questions and then listening actively to what your clients are saying and not saying.

Lead them through a conversation where you seek to understand what's going on for them. Try to uncover details of their experience and the symptoms and problems that triggered them to start shopping.

What will it cost them if they do nothing? What will they gain if they make the purchase? Their stories will tell you volumes about what's motivating them.

In marketing and advertising, you can't speak directly to people, so you need to conduct market research. You need to develop personas, and empathy maps, to inform your message and creative concepts. The goal is to speak directly to your target client as if you know them and empathise with them.

The Call to Action

It's challenging to make an emotional connection with someone unless you know them. You build personas and empathy maps for each buyer type to make writing directly to that person easier.
Don't get stuck on demographic descriptions such as age or income. They are important for segmentation and targeting, but people's fears, goals, and motivations are far more useful.

If you're not fluent in emotional language, type "list of feelings" or "list of emotions" into your search engine for ideas.

Use an empathy map framework to get into your clients' heads, then select the words that describe how they feel before and after buying from you. Use the map as an emotional profile and then test your assumptions with some existing clients. Let them share and help you understand them at a more intimate level.

Your communication will improve and your message will have a greater impact and resonance when you practise being affective.

Thoughts and Action Planning

Now build upon the persona work you did in the last chapter. You want to create an emotional context.

1. Why does your offering matter to your persona in their role?

2. What is personally at stake for them? Their company? Job security? A raise or promotion? Pain relief?

3. How anxiety-provoking is your topic area? Do they know the subject matter well, or is it unfamiliar and intimidating?

4. Where does their ego, pride, or self-image fit into their purchase?

5. How do they feel about their situation now? Use emotional language to reflect on how they feel.

6. How will they feel if your solution saves the day for them or makes a huge difference?

7. Look at your advertising, your sales literature, and your proposals. How well do they fit the profiles you just developed?

Resources for Being Affective

Emotion Word Lists

One of the most challenging aspects of being affective is developing an emotional vocabulary. Here are a couple of resources for expanding your emotional language.

https://wire.wisc.edu/quizzesnmore/emotionwords.aspx

http://www.psychpage.com/learning/library/assess/feelings.html

Relevant Books To Review
SPIN Selling
by Neil Rackham

Applied Empathy
The New Language of Leadership
by Michael Ventura

Empathy Maps
Step-By-Step Guide
by Robert Curedale

Words That Change Minds:
The 14 Patterns For Mastering The Language of Influence
by Shelle Rose Charvet

—— BEING ——
ATTRACTIVE

Expressing Authentically

"Your smile is a messenger of your goodwill."

Dale Carnegie

THE DESIGN STAGE

BEING ATTRACTIVE

About Being Attractive

The most immediate reaction to the word attractive is to assume good looks. Thankfully looks are only part of the equation. Sure, you want to make a good first impression. You want to look the part and not turn people off. But looks alone are rarely enough to make it through the first date, let alone an enduring customer relationship.

Confidence is always key, as is attitude, listening, authenticity, integrity, reliability, transparency, respect, grace, generosity, charm, and more.

Being attractive is knowing who you are, respecting yourself and others, then fully living into your unique possibility with no apologies.

This is not arrogance or selfishness. Those are not attractive. What I'm talking about is owning who you are and living into the possibility you represent.

To be attractive, you need to know who you are as a leader, as a product, as a company, and as an opportunity.

In marketing terms, this conversation is about your brand and what you make it mean.

No, your brand is not your logo. Your brand is the cumulative experience people have of you over time. It's who clients perceive you to be, based on their experience of you. Your reputation is another way of saying it.

When people start speaking well of you to others and promoting you as worthy of their attention, time, money, and trust, you have become attractive and desirable.

Why Is Being Attractive Necessary?

The simple answer is because you want to grow your business with the least amount of cost and effort. It is far easier to be attractive and well thought of than it is to recover from not meeting expectations.

If we look at the opposite of attractive to make the point clear, we're talking about being repulsive and causing people to avoid you. I realise we're talking about extremes, but the last thing you want in business is to be repulsive.

Repulsive behaviours include things like being arrogant, selfish, impatient, unreliable, negative, unpredictable, uncaring, disrespectful, intolerant, all the way to being racist, sexist, and abusive.

It's easy to say you're not abusive, for example, but it is not so easy to never be rude or disrespectful. These acts can seem like minor relationship infractions, but they have the same repulsive effect and undermine your efforts. They diminish your brand and make you less attractive.

The Costs of Not Being Attractive

To overcome a lack of attractiveness, you need to compensate in other ways. Compensations are expensive, unnatural, and forced.

Compensations are things like heavy advertising, promotions, frequent discounting, and resorting to gimmicks and tricks to bring people in and make sales.

Compensations cost you on the front-end with additional expenses and on the backend with lower margin sales.

How to Practise Being Attractive

You practise being attractive by setting a standard you, your target audience, and your competitors all agree upon.

Consider the difference between a one star and a five star hotel. The one star hotel gives you somewhere to sleep that is warm, has running water, and a door that locks. The price is low, and that is what you expect from a one star hotel.

At a five star hotel, you'll pay a hefty sum for an experience where no subtle detail is left unattended. You can expect each aspect of your experience to exceed expectations. Five star hotels pay attention to quality, style, cleanliness, comfort, convenience, customer service, and more.

Before you can practise being attractive, you need to define the target you're shooting for. You need to design the experience your clients expect.

The Call to Action

What agreement are you making with your customers? Are you setting a one star or a five star expectation or somewhere in between? Do your homework and decide what's authentic.

What's going to make you attractive to your target audience? What sets you apart from your competition and allows you to make a profit?

Don't guess. Shop your competitors, talk to potential clients, consider your offering, and decide what's authentic and economically viable, then decide.

If you're a three star business, own it. Be the best three star business you can be. Don't try to be a five star operation, because you won't have the margins to support it.

Being attractive is ultimately about meeting the expectations of your marketplace, in a way that is authentic and sustainable.

Thoughts and Action Planning

1. Who's the most attractive competitor in your category?

2. What makes them so attractive? Is it their marketing? Their packaging? Their customer service? Do they have a great office with amazing perks? Is it their reputation, awards, events they host, high-profile clients? Try to put your finger on it.

3. Where do you fit on these same dimensions?

4. Which factors matter to you, to your customers, and your staff?

5. Which factors do you have the resources to control? Where can you step-up and do better?

6. If you had to pick the top three factors to work on, which would you choose? What would you do to enhance each of them?

7. If you could design your customers' experience as people move through your business, how would it go?

Resources for Being Attractive

How To Win Friends & Influence People
by Dale Carnegie

The User Experience Team of One
by Leah Buley

The Ten Principles Behind Great Customer Experiences
by Matt Watkinson

Designing Experiences
by J Robert Rossman PhD

The Art of Authenticity
Tools to Become an Authentic Leader and Your Best Self
by Karissa Thaker

The Experience
The 5 Principles of Disney Service and Relationship Excellence
by Bruce Loeffler & Brian T. Church

—— BEING ——
COMPELLING

Creating Urgency

"The best way to persuade people is with your ears by listening to them."

Dean Rusk

THE DESIGN STAGE

BEING COMPELLING

About Being Compelling

Being compelling is about evoking a sense of urgency and creating a need to take immediate action. The absence of action should feel like a missed opportunity or an increased risk of failure.

Why Is Being Compelling Necessary?

When you're investing in sales and marketing, you expect a return on your investment. To get a return on investment, you need to get people to act now.

Unfortunately, people are short on attention. They are impulsive and easily distracted by all kinds of conflicting demands on their time.

If they don't act now, how long will it take them to come back around to take action? It's hard to say, but it could be hours, days, weeks, or never.

Your primary means of getting anyone to act is to be as compelling as possible.

The Costs of Not Being Compelling

You need to be compelling because now is where you make sales. Without being compelling, the name of the game changes to persistent follow-up. Follow-up may be essential for sales, but it is always more costly than when clients take immediate action.

It is challenging enough to cover the cost of promotion but adding the high cost of human follow-up takes an extra chunk off your profit margin.

How to Practise Being Compelling

The easiest way to be compelling is to have your prospects show up with an urgent need. Then it's not just you being compelling; their situation is compelling them too.

Then there are situations where the client has a compelling need, but they don't know it. In my experience, this is the most common scenario. If you can bring their urgency to the surface, people are more likely to act.

The third scenario is where you manufacture urgency to elicit a reaction.

The first scenario is proactive and is about marketing to trigger events. You promote into scenarios where there is natural or inherent urgency like when you are selling a house. Once you've found a house, there is an inherent urgency to line up mortgage financing.

The second scenario is similar. You market to a segment which has a very high probability of needing you. For example, business owners have a high likelihood of needing communication effectiveness training. The problem is that many don't realise it. You practise being compelling by helping them to recognise the problem, the damage it is causing, the implications of inaction, and the benefits of corrective action. You compel them to action by making it abundantly clear what it will cost them if they do nothing.

The third way is to manufacture urgency with:

- time-limited offers
- product scarcity (only five left)

What you're doing is tapping into their fear of missing out.

You can also eliminate their reasons for not acting now. You can:

- eliminate ambiguity / clarify the offer
- reduce buyer risk
- proactively address fears with FAQs
- offer social proof with case studies and testimonials
- offer financing or a mix of payment options
- clarify your return policy
- offer a warranty period

Ideally, you try to create urgency and eliminate obstacles to "yes".

The Call to Action

If you're going to make sales and marketing investments to grow your company, you need to understand your clients' needs, fears and motivations. You need to find a way to create urgency without significant impact on your profit margin.

Thoughts and Action Planning

1. Why do people normally buy from you? What are their motivations?

2. What are the natural trigger events causing people to need to buy what you offer?

3. Scarcity is an important trigger. If you have a limited supply, people who are on the fence may act. How can you create scarcity?

4. Bundling your offering with related offerings for a combined discount can also create urgency. Who could you collaborate with to add a zero-cost bonus to your offering?

5. Convenience is important. How can you make acting now the most convenient option?

6. Proactive objection handling. What can you do, to alleviate the fear of taking action?

Resources for Being Compelling

Shift

Harness The Trigger Events That Turn Prospects into Customers
by Craig Elias and Tibor Shanto

Words That Change Minds:

The 14 Patterns for Mastering the Language of Influence
by Shelle Rose Charvet

SPIN Selling

by Neil Rackham

BEING
KNOWABLE

Achieving Transparency

"Speak the truth. Transparency breeds legitimacy."
John C. Maxwell

THE DESIGN STAGE

BEING KNOWABLE

About Being Knowable

Being knowable is about transparency. It's about allowing people access to information about you, what you're about, your mission, vision, values, and the story that led you here.

It's surprising how often I run into people who are so concerned about privacy, that they will not share even a hint of who they are in their marketing materials.

"It's hard to read a closed book."

Why Is Being Knowable Necessary?

Being knowable is a precursor to trust. Think about it; how do you have a relationship with someone you don't know?

What's the first thing people do when they meet someone? They talk and get to know each other. Then afterwards, they check out their online presence. Depending on your business or how old your target audience is, they will expect to find your company and you personally online.

They will look for your website. They will check you out on Facebook or LinkedIn. If they're younger, they will look for you on Instagram. The mix of online platforms is always changing, and there is no right or wrong. What matters is that you choose a mix and develop an online presence that makes sense for your target audience.

A medical clinic will have a completely different online presence than a law firm or an engineering company.

What's important is the need for clients to get to know you. It is human nature and a necessary step to weed out the pretenders and the predators from those worthy of attention and trust.

The Costs of Not Being Knowable

Making it difficult to get to know you and your company costs you time and money. Simply put, it takes longer to develop trust and goodwill as a closed book than an open one.

Being private, aloof, mysterious, or inapproachable has its place. It might be appropriate as a private individual; however, as a business or business owner, you need to allow people a glimpse of who you are.

This is particularly true for Generation X and even more so for Millennials who grew up with the Internet and who, as a group, tend to share everything.

People expect you to share and be authentic. Likewise, people distrust those who lack transparency.

How to Practise Being Knowable

How you practise being knowable depends greatly on your situation, your profession, your role, your brand, and the image you're trying to cultivate.

Allowing yourself and your company to be known is not about sharing information freely, it's about crafting an image and a voice with style, intent, candour, and reservation.

A little well-crafted information goes a long way. The irony about being knowable is that people are as disinterested as they are interested. They don't want to know everything; they just want enough information to validate their instincts about you.

If you tell people too much, they'll shut down and get turned off.

There is an art to being transparent, interesting, knowable, and measured at the same time.

What's an appropriate level of disclosure? How will you help people get to know you and your company? These are questions you need to consider.

The Call to Action

There are many components to being knowable online as a business or as a professional.

Your name/company name is first. Use your full name or your tradename the way it appears on your business card or advertising so people will recognise it. Obvious, I know.

The first component after your name is your photography. You need to show people who you are with a headshot or so-called hero shot of your product or business. It is part of your first impression online, and it needs to be good.

Please do not use a selfie or a Walmart headshot or anything from your cellphone, unless it's very good. Do not underestimate the power and importance of your photography. It is a very powerful first impression mechanism. Hire a professional for your main photos. These will be some of your highest visibility marketing elements, so make them good.

Next is your title or positioning line—this is vital as well. These five words need to tell people why they should keep reading. Why are you relevant to them? What role do you play? You have three seconds to get their attention. How are you going to position your business or yourself?

About You has two parts. The first paragraph should be short, to the point and tell people what you want them to know in two to three well-written, punchy lines.

If people only read your name, look at your photo, tagline, and the first paragraph of your intro, and then leave, will they get the essential story?

The second half of your intro can be longer and more detailed. It should reiterate and expand on what you just said. Try to answer the questions: who are we, who do we serve, what problem do we solve or what opportunity do we create, and why us versus the competition?

This is the starting point. If you do these first few things well, you'll appease 90% of your audience. When they check you out, you will have made sure they got the right first impression.

After these basics, consider the questions they are likely to ask, and answer them. Cover the basics using the who, what, when, where, how, and why structure.

Next are your stories, and there can be several to tell.

You can tell your origin story. You can explain why you invented your product or why you started your business. You can share client stories. Alternatively, you can cover important news about what you are doing, or the charities you support.

All these stories help to make you relatable and allow people to feel like they have a sense of who they're dealing with.

Not everyone will read all this material, but it's important to offer it for those who go looking.

Thoughts and Action Planning

1. How easy do you make it for people to get to know you and your business?

2. Do you have a simple and compelling introduction that positions you the way you want people to think of you?

3. Have you developed profiles or business pages on LinkedIn, Facebook, Alignable, Google My Business and other popular social and directory sites?

4. Do you have an About Us section on your website? It is often a highly-visited page.

5. Have you shared your origin story, explaining why you do what you do and why it's important to you?

6. Have you shared your mission, vision, and values?

7. Do you share any news about what's going on for you and your company?

Resources for Being Knowable

Resources that address this Way of Being include:

The Hero Shot – Video Tutorial

https://digitalartthatrocks.com/blog/2018/2/12/the-hero-shot-commercial-photographer-and-digital-artist-brian-rodgers-jr-product-photography

Positioning
The Battle For Your Mind
By Al Ries and Jack Trout

The Transparency Sale
How Unexpected Honest and Understanding the Buying Brain Can Transform Your Results
by Todd Caponi

Storynomics
Story-Driven Marketing in the Post-Advertising World
by Robert McKee

THE
BUILD STAGE

Enabling Growth

THE BUILD STAGE

The Ways of Being in the build stage are about operational excellence. As in the design stage, the Ways are not mutually exclusive. You can work on sets of Ways together.

These Ways include:

> Being Responsive – meeting expectation
>
> Being Buyable – easing the purchase path
>
> Being Systematic – implementing best practices
>
> Being Informed – tracking performance
>
> Being Effective – ensuring sustainability
>
> Being Scalable – preparing for growth

For new and small companies, the build stage is about putting systems and processes together to help your business operate and scale.

For mature companies, you use these Ways to gauge the performance of existing systems.

Problems you find are often the result of Way misalignments. Once you identify misalignments, you can realign your practices to optimise performance.

— BEING —
RESPONSIVE

Meeting Expectations

"Speed, agility and responsiveness are the keys to future success."

Anita Roddick

THE BUILD STAGE

BEING RESPONSIVE

About Being Responsive

Being responsive on a human scale is about your readiness and capacity to anticipate client needs in a proactive and timely manner. Being responsive is different from being reactive in an important way. Whereas being responsive is about readiness and preparedness, being reactive is about frantically putting out fires and dealing with a lack of preparedness. Both are situationally necessary but being responsive reduces how much reacting you need to do.

A timely manner is an important dimension of Being Responsive. How responsive do you need to be? What is the scale and urgency you need to prepare for?

As I write this passage, several hurricanes and typhoons are menacing the globe. I can't help but relate this discussion to the emergency response preparations and the actual responses consecutively underway.

If you live in an area ravaged by severe storms, how important is the level of preparation by government, utilities, and aid organisations? What scale of response will they need to mount when they are called upon? How quickly can they scale their response by mobilising additional resources when faced with catastrophic situations?

Your business may not be as life and death as what I'm describing, but perhaps it's mission-critical to your clients. Are you reacting, or are you prepared to respond and to scale your response when necessary?

In a local example, my grocer guarantees every checkout lane will be open on the weekends to lessen the strain on everyone's patience. That's a solid example of being responsive to client needs.

In website terms, being responsive refers to whether your website can reconfigure content to meet the needs of the many screen sizes it will encounter.

How responsive are you? Are you prepared to deal with unanticipated demand or mission-critical situations?

Why Is Being Responsive Necessary?

Your responsiveness is a central aspect of your brand promise and a tangible means for your clients to measure your performance against your peers.

Part of who you present your company to be is based on your ability to meet clients' needs under normal and even somewhat extreme circumstances.

The easier you are tripped up and shown to be unprepared, the looser your grip on your clients and the more vulnerable you are to the competition. Being responsive is necessary to survive and thrive in a dynamic and unpredictable world.

The Costs of Not Being Responsive

The costs of not being responsive are threefold. The most obvious result is missing out on opportunities due to your inability to respond.

The less obvious result is the harm done to your reputation.

The third and most immediate result is the chaos, energy and costs expended, while reacting or trying to react versus being prepared to respond effectively.

One of the barriers that prevent people from advertising or engaging in public relations is their inability to deal with the volume of opportunities these activities create.

The window of opportunity for most new business is short. You need to be prepared to respond to opportunities in advance, or you may miss the opportunities entirely.

Not being able to respond to opportunities is one of the most troublesome challenges you face when investing in marketing. If you can't follow-up on the opportunities you create, there's no point in creating them.

How to Practise Being Responsive

The US Department of Homeland Security / Federal Emergency Management Agency model (US – DHS / FEMA) is engaged in "a continuous cycle of planning, organising, training, equipping, exercising, evaluating, and taking corrective action to ensure effective coordination during incident response." https://www.dhs.gov/plan-and-prepare-disasters

FEMA is dealing with large scale, life and death situations, which are different from the average small business reality. However, there is nothing in their process that is not scalable to the small business level.

In a marketing context, we talk about the customer journey as a series of use cases, which are not dissimilar from an incident response framework. The question is whether you know what to anticipate and are prepared to respond to it.

In this context, your ability to be responsive begins with your understanding of your client's needs.

Your customer's journey refers to the long-term journey people make through your company, as they endeavour to get their needs met over time. Their journey can be easy, enjoyable, and shareworthy, or it can be a frustrating nightmare and the source of epic fail posts and negative reviews.

Use cases are typically shorter-term, pragmatic sequences where someone attempts to get something specific accomplished. It's a pattern you follow to complete a task or reach a decision.

For example, what are the steps involved in getting through your retail checkout process?

Each use case can be modelled with simple tools like flowcharts, or mapped in detail with swim lane diagrams or a series of user interfaces.

A customer's journey is made up of many different use cases. Think about how many different ways you interact with clients. At the very least, there's a sales use case, a payment use case, a customer service use case and more. What happens in each interaction? What are your client's expectations?

How prepared are you to ensure your client's experience is one of ease, grace, and professionalism along their path through your business?

The Call to Action

Get into your customer's shoes and walk that mile. Map out your customer's journey. Identify and map out each of your customer's use cases.

Then do the planning, organising, training, equipping and practising necessary to be responsive to your client's needs.

Thoughts and Action Planning

1. If you had a sudden spike in business from marketing, how prepared are you to handle it?

2. How much new business can you handle, before your systems and people falter?

3. Have you mapped your customer's purchase process? What are the gaps or most likely problem areas?

4. What is your post-sale process?

5. What is the state of your customer journey mapping? Is it non-existent, sketched out, or mapped in detail?

6. What are the gaps and pinch points in your customer journey map? Where is your production capacity the least scalable?

7. What is the one thing you could do to increase your responsiveness at each pinch point?

Resources for Being Responsive

Developing and Maintaining Emergency Operations Plans
https://www.fema.gov/media-library/assets/documents/25975

Visit and explore the Responsive.org website

Watch this short video on the need for responsiveness
https://youtu.be/jnmr8zvomE8

Responsive
What It Takes to Create a Thriving Organization
by Robin Peter Zander

State of Readiness
Operational Excellence as a Precursor to Becoming a High-Performance Organization
by Joseph F. Paris Jr.

— BEING —
BUYABLE

Easing the Purchase Path

*"…understand how the customer wants to buy
and help them to do so."*
Bryan Eisenberg

THE BUILD STAGE

BEING BUYABLE

About Being Buyable

This chapter is not about being susceptible to bribery. This conversation is about making your business easy to buy from.

Being easy to buy from is about:

1. Having what your clients need and want
2. Supporting your client's decision to buy from you
3. Making the transaction easy to complete, logistically
4. Ensuring the exchange is completed effectively

Why Is Being Buyable Necessary?

The rationale is simple enough. The harder you make it for people to deal with you, the fewer people will do it.

The easier you make it for people to overcome their fear and reluctance, the more likely they'll be to proceed.

The more difficult you make it to buy from you, the more effort you and your client expend negotiating the transaction. The longer it takes, the more likely they are not to complete the transaction.

Why? Because things come up and priorities change quickly. Other people get involved and complicate the decision-making process. People lose interest, or they have time to comparison shop.

With people's declining attention spans and lack of patience, you need to make it easy to buy or you'll make fewer sales.

The Costs of Not Being Buyable

In a retail context, people leave your store without making a purchase.

In a complex sale, your sales team/consultants spend extra time and effort answering questions and compensating for an inefficient process. Every extra step required increases your average cost of sale.

The costs of being difficult to buy from include:

- reducing your sales conversion rates
- elongating your sales cycle times
- increasing your average cost of sale
- frustrating your clients and staff
- reducing your competitiveness
- reducing your profit margins

How to Practise Being Buyable

There are four main areas to focus on:

1. Having what your clients need and want
2. Supporting your client's decision to buy from you
3. Simplifying purchase logistics
4. Ensuring the exchange is completed effectively

Let's break each factor down.

Having What Your Clients Need and Want

This factor involves knowing your customers and anticipating their needs with your product and service selection.

It involves maintaining appropriate inventory levels, so you have what people need when they need it.

It involves making sure your clients can find your products with signage, browsing, or search efforts.

Marketing can often drive people into your business, but you can't make a sale if you don't have what they came for, or they can't find it.

Supporting Your Client's Decision to Buy

Supporting the decision process has many components as well. It often starts with the availability of information about the product or service.

Sometimes, in the interest of design and simplicity, you pare down product information too far. Vital details are lost. There's nothing but hype and insufficient details to answer basic product questions.

From your promotion to your packaging and supportive documentation, are you making the vital statistics available to support your buyer's decision process?

The vital data is situation-specific, so you need to know what data your clients will look for.

I'm a technical guy who buys technical products, and I'm often frustrated by a lack of basic specifications. If I don't know them, I'm not buying.

The same is true for reviews. I prefer to read a few before buying things.

The target client, along with the size and complexity of the sale, will dictate what you need to provide. The point is, you need to know how your clients make decisions and then make it easy for them to access what they want.

Simplifying Purchase Logistics

Purchase logistics can be as simple as a checkout counter or as complicated as a pile of forms and contracts to review and complete.

Often the process is one-sided to support the needs of the business and less about the purchaser's needs. The challenge is to look at it from both perspectives.

What are you asking your clients to endure, to be able to buy from you?

Sometimes you can ask too much from people, and they'll bale out, due to frustration or time delays.

I know a long line-up at checkout is often enough for me to abandon my cart and go elsewhere.

I worked with an online retailer who built a 13-step checkout process, that almost no one could tolerate. They thought that breaking the process down into small steps would help users, but it cut their sales down to nothing.

When they redesigned the process to five steps, their conversions increased significantly (from less than 0.1% to nearly 14%).

There are many factors to consider, from your customer's point of view:

- perception of security
- payment options
- presence of a privacy policy
- shipping, delivery times, and options
- warranty and return periods
- simplicity of your agreements
- degree of legalese in your contract

Ensuring the Exchange is Completed Effectively

Once an agreement is signed or the buy now button is pressed, what happens next?

Is it a frustrating experience, or does it all go swimmingly?

Is the post-sale process thoughtful and efficient? Can clients reach you if there's a question or a problem?

Is there any post-sale follow-up? Is there a "thanks for the business" gesture, or a satisfaction survey?

Expectations differ, depending on the nature of the sale. What thought have you given to the post-sale experience?

What's the likelihood of a repeat sale, if the experience is less than expected? What can you do to capitalise on this opportunity?

The Call to Action

Being easy to buy from is not a small undertaking. If you operate a professional service business, sell intangibles, or deal in large and complex transactions, the process can be complicated.

The starting point is to walk the process yourself and experience what your clients go through.

Shop your competitors as well for comparison.

Consider calling a few clients for feedback on their experience. You might wish to use a third party to conduct the interviews so people will be more forthcoming.

If you sell through a website, you'll have all kinds of data to see how people are moving through your sales process. It's important to ask the question, How do we make it easy to buy from us? How do we facilitate our customers, so they feel good about the experience?

In my experience, being buyable is one of the most important factors to gain control over. It's complex with a lot of moving parts, but it's a very high leverage area to focus on.

Thoughts and Action Planning

Becoming easy to buy from has many facets.

1. Start by mapping out the client's purchase process, from promotion to post-sale.

2. See what data you have on traffic volumes, purchase path analysis, heat mapping, conversion rates, average costs per sales, and customer satisfaction. What is your data telling you?

3. Shop your process as well as your competitors. What are the biggest impediments? How are your competitors ahead of you?

4. How many steps are there in the purchase process? How many steps can you eliminate?

5. What information is essential to the sale? Is it easily accessible?

6. Would special terms, financing, or payment options increase sales?

7. What is your post-sale experience? Are you tripping up at the finishing line? What can you do to finish well?

Resources for Being Buyable

Why We Buy
The Science Of Shopping
by Paco Underhill

Don't Make Me Think, Revisited
A Common Sense Approach To Web Usability
by Steve Krug

— BEING —
SYSTEMATIC

Implementing Best Practices

"You can only elevate performance
by elevating the entire system."
W. Edward Deming

THE BUILD STAGE

BEING SYSTEMATIC

About Being Systematic

Investorwords.com defines a systematic approach as: "… a process used to determine the viability of a project or procedure based on the experiential application of clearly defined and repeatable steps and an evaluation of the outcomes. The goal of a systematic approach is to identify the most efficient means to generate consistent, optimum results."

The core ideas in this definition are the clearly defined, repeatable steps to produce consistent and optimal results. How well does this definition fit your business development efforts? Be honest.

Many of the business owners I've met will shrug and admit they are not systematic with their business development efforts. The most common reason shared is because they don't understand marketing as a system. It occurs to them more like a to-do list of independent tasks.

Why Is Being Systematic Necessary?

If we return to the definition, you want to be systematic to produce consistent and optimal results. In practical terms, you want to drive sales and generate a reasonable rate of return on your marketing and promotional investments.

The repeatability component is equally important. Without the process being repeatable, you can't rely on it.

In addition to being more efficient, systems allow your marketing to be:

- more consistent and reliable
- easier to track and manage
- easier to streamline and automate

The Costs of Not Being Systematic

You can sum up the main implications of not being systematic in four concepts: inconsistent, unreliable, capacity constrained, and inefficient.

You can translate these concepts to higher costs, lower quality, and being less competitive.

You can also sum this up into a lack of investor confidence. You'll be less confident investing in marketing if there is no reliable system to generate a decent rate of return.

How to Practise Being Systematic

The practice of being systematic begins with being clear on your financial constraints, your goals, and what you want your customer's journey to look like.

What you're designing is a way to manage every client interaction from advertising through to repeat business. You're scripting your relationship development scenarios.

You start by mapping how your system works. You define the actors, the inputs and interfaces; you develop procedures, decision logic, templates, and internal and external performance objectives. You also identify points in the process with high leverage to track and report on.

You don't have to take on the whole system at once. You can break down your system into subsystems and component mechanisms. The point is to take a long-term view of things and recognise how all the parts fit together to create the outcomes you need.

What Normally Happens

Unfortunately, what we see most often are two alternate patterns: Random acts of marketing and to-do list marketing.

Random Acts of Marketing

Random acts of marketing are exactly what they sound like: chaotic. You try a bit of this; you experiment with that, or you get sold on the benefits of some new technology. You don't have a plan, so doing something is better than nothing.

You might say "hope is the strategy" and "distraction and wishful thinking" is the plan.

This approach produces as well as you might expect.

To-do List Marketing

To-do List marketing is more common in larger companies, with an annual marketing budget. Each year, funds get allocated to independent marketing activities in a shopping list-like manner.

In many instances, there is a great deal of effort put into the careful allocation of funds. There is often a marketing manager in place, who consults with media planners and sales representatives for help deciding what to buy. It all sounds perfectly reasonable. The individual expenses all make sense as stand-alone purchases.

So What's the Problem?

The problem is a lack of context. Without understanding marketing as a system, it's difficult to pinpoint problems.

You're more likely to allocate funds to squeaky wheels, pet projects and "nice to haves", because you can't see where the money really needs to go.

To-do list marketing can produce abysmal results for several years because performance tracking is limited or non-existent. The only reason it's allowed to continue is because people have such low expectations of marketing. It's often just assumed you need to spend X per cent of revenue per year on marketing and you hope for the best.

I've seen companies spend $500,000 per year this way because there is no marketing system awareness and no performance tracking.

Where are you on this continuum? Is hope your strategy? Are you to-do list marketing, or are you building and refining a system to produce results reliably?

The Call to Action

To break out of these dysfunctional marketing behaviours, the first thing to do is map your customer's journey through your business. Break the journey up into segments where conversion rates (decision points) occur.

Map the journey from the first sale, through repeat sales and on to loyal long-term clients.

Look at your infrastructure, your computer systems and software, and evaluate whether they can communicate with each other. If you have old or proprietary systems, it might be time to upgrade.

Next, look at your team and determine if they're prepared to support your transition. Do you have the right people on the bus? What types of training will your people need?

Developing a system is not an overnight project. Systems are something you'll develop and refine over time.

Once you see the system and understand how it works relative to the current state, you'll wonder how you ever did it any other way.

Thoughts and Action Planning

1. Start with your client's journey through your business. Map the sequence from their first exposure to you, all the way to year two in your relationship.
    a. Keep the path at a high-level to start
    b. Map the current processes
    c. Then map an ideal state (consider using a swim lane diagram for this)
2. Where are the gaps in the process? What steps do you need to add or eliminate?
3. Locate each significant conversion event along the path and see if you can track these conversion rates.
4. What's happening at each conversion point? Are there forms, templates, and supporting documents?
5. What software is in place along your customer's journey (websites, email, point of sale, customer relationship management, service tickets, estimating, accounting, etc.)?
6. Will your software integrate with other systems (open data model, API or data export)?
7. Consider whether a marketing automation system would help you be more systematic in how you manage customer relationships.

Resources for Being Systematic

The Essential Deming: Leadership Principles
by W. Edwards Deming

The Fifth Discipline
The Art and Practice of the Learning Organization
by Peter Senge

Learning Systems Thinking
by Wallace Wright

Systems Thinking Speech
https://www.youtube.com/watch?v=EbLh7rZ3rhU
by Russel Ackoff

Process Mapping, Process Improvement, and Process Management
A Practical Guide to Enhancing Work and Information Flow
by Dan Madison

— BEING — INFORMED

Tracking Performance

"In God We Trust; all others bring data."
W. Edward Deming

THE BUILD STAGE

BEING INFORMED

About Being Informed

Being informed is about knowing how effectively your business development system is working. How well your system is working means different things to different stakeholders.

You measure performance with hierarchies of key performance indicators. The highest-level indicators focus on the big picture. There are more detailed metrics for sales and marketing directors, and even more detailed metrics are used by analysts and department managers.

What gets measured generally relates to the economic performance of the system, rate of client acquisition, retention rates, lifetime value, customer satisfaction, and a host of others.

Why Is Being Informed Necessary?

Without meaningful feedback on how well your business development system is working, you can't manage it. Without feedback, you're right back to to-do lists and random acts of marketing.

You have to best guess, make assumptions, and hope what you're doing makes sense. But you never really know, which lends itself either to taking big risks or playing it safe. Neither option works particularly well.

The Costs of Not Being Informed

At a high level, the cost of not being informed is waste. A lot of waste.

More specifically, it translates into a lack of certainty and commitment, fear to act, less assertive marketing, lost opportunities, and a lack of responsiveness. In summary: slower growth and lower margins.

How to Practise Being Informed

Practising being informed is a matter of having gauges installed at key points along the customer's journey. You monitor conversion performance at each point (tracking how many people make it from one stage to the next).

Anything internet based has become relatively easy to track. There's almost too much feedback available that you need to wade through.

Anything not digital gets challenging because people are involved.

The systems to focus on include:

- social media posts and advertising
- reviews and customer service metrics
- search-demand trends
- search engine web master accounts
- telephone systems
- sales and opportunity management systems
- point of sale systems
- customer databases
- help desk ticketing systems

You want gauges at every significant touchpoint along your customer's journey.

Ideally, you're looking at your internal systems not just with an eye for functionality, but for their connectivity. How easy do they make it for you to integrate them with other systems and to access your data? How easily will they integrate with your website and industry-standard tracking tools?

It's not enough for systems to serve their core purpose because you end up with information silos that make it difficult to access, integrate, and analyse your data.

The Call to Action

For many people, the easiest place to start is with your website and Google Analytics. Google Analytics is a free website tracking application. It's a great place to start learning about marketing and customer performance metrics.

What's important is to learn how to segment your data and focus on key performance indicators, rather than getting lost in information overload.

To use the system, you need to learn what's relevant and important.

For Example:

If you operate a local business in North America, do you care how many people from Russia visit your website? No, so get rid of everyone from outside your trade area.

Do total visits matter or are you more interested in the number of unique, new, or repeat visitors?

What percentage of visitors (from within your trade area) bounce off your website without looking around? What percentage engage with your content and spend time on your website?

How many people download something, contact you, sign up for updates, and buy something? What's the average unit cost per goal completion from a given advertising source? Are your average costs sustainable, or do they exceed your client's average lifetime value?

What percentage of new leads result in sales? What percentage of new clients return to buy again? What's the client churn rate and the average lifetime value of a new client in their first year?

The list of things to measure is endless. What you need to determine is what's relevant to your business and start to use that information to make decisions faster and more strategically.

Thoughts and Action Planning

1. Start with the basics. What is the average value of a new client's first purchase?
2. What's the most you can pay for that sale without losing money?
3. What percentage of new clients buy a second time?
4. What's the average lifetime value of a client in their first year?
5. What percentage of first-year clients do you retain into year two?
6. What are you willing to invest in acquiring a new client?
7. What is it currently costing you to acquire a new customer?
8. Which promotional channels produce the lowest cost clients?

Once you get your head into these core metrics, you can dig into your marketing data and optimise the heck out of everything.

It just takes some practice to learn how to access and make sense of your data so you can be informed.

Resources for Being Informed

Measure What Matters
by John Doerr

Key Performance Indicators
The 75 Measures Every Manager Needs to Know
by Bernard Marr

Sales Funnel
Management for Small Business Owners in 2019
by Mark Warner

Google Analytics Demystified
by Alexa L. Mokalis, Joel J. Davis

BEING
EFFECTIVE

Ensuring Sustainability

"Never neglect an opportunity for improvement."
William Jones

THE BUILD STAGE

BEING EFFECTIVE

About Being Effective

Once you're tracking performance regularly, you become informed. Assuming you're tracking the right things, you'll know if what you are doing is sustainable.

Albert Einstein famously said that "doing the same thing over and over again and expecting a different result, is the definition of insanity".

However, once you see that what you're doing is not working, you can do it differently. You can modify the underperforming elements of your system.

Being effective is about living in a state of continuous improvement, where you work first to achieve sustainability, and then push towards high-performance.

Why Is Being Effective Necessary?

Let's be clear; if your business development efforts do not help you get and keep new clients at a profit, they are not working.

Until you get your business development system working, you're depleting your reserves. In the startup community, people often describe your reserve funds as your runway. Your plane has a limited length of runway before it needs to fly, or it will crash and burn.

Here's the problem: you don't pay attention to your information. It's likely you actively avoid it. Why? Because the truth hurts, and you don't want to see it.

Even when the information is right in front of you, you'll often distract yourself from the truth, rather than deal with the problem.

In organisations large and small, ignorance is bliss and denial is not just a big river in Africa. Okay bad joke, but you get the point.

As a society, we don't face facts, and we certainly don't leap into action, even when the situation is dire.

There are plenty of examples of this:

- Gun violence in the US
- Pollution and climate change
- The obesity epidemic
- The opioid crisis
- Plastics in the environment
- Pesticides killing our critical pollinators (bees)

I think it's safe to say that, as a society, we don't act upon information. We do what we want to do until there is a dire crisis, and even then, we resist change.

If you want to be effective, you need more than insightful feedback. You need to be willing to face hard facts. You need to get your ego out of the way and be willing to do things you don't want to do. Are you up for that?

The Costs of Not Being Effective

The main cost of not being effective at business development is playing it small. If you're not willing to track and manage performance, you'll hold back and invest slowly and cautiously.

There are plenty of hungry business owners who'll gladly dive into their data and tweak and adjust their business model relentlessly. What they're building is their confidence to invest.

It's happening all around you with so-called high-performance competitors, the internet of things, industry disruptors, and the gig economy.

You may not want to be an industry disruptor, but not pushing hard to create an effective marketing and selling system is going to leave you behind your progressive and data-savvy peers.

How to Practise Being Effective

Spencer Johnson wrote a fabulous book called *Who Moved My Cheese?* in which he explores our tendencies to resist change. It's a parable about four mice dealing with an inconvenient truth. The cheese is gone, and it's not coming back. The book explores how we adapt to change—by resisting it or by accepting the change and moving forward actively.

It's a great book that takes about an hour to read. I guarantee you will see yourself and everyone you know in the four characters; Hem, Haw, Sniff, and Scurry.

The book is an excellent catalyst for contemplating how you respond to information and inconvenient truths.

The good news is the hardest part of being effective at anything is deciding to commit to it. Once you've committed, you can get busy becoming effective.

In his book, *The Fifth Discipline*, Peter Senge argues the solution to becoming effective is to become a learning organisation. The book is compelling if weighty, but let's focus on his rule #8 that states "small changes can produce big results".

He talks about identifying points of leverage, where changes made with minimal effort can lead to lasting, significant improvement.

Being effective starts with being informed, but the information alone is not enough. You need to put it to use. You need to set up and run experiments to see what works best.

Make sure you're focused on the highest points of leverage in your marketing, sales and service processes.

Once you know where to focus, and have clear and specific success criteria, you can get busy testing scenarios to see what works.

The Call to Action

One of the most compelling first steps I recommend is a marketing audit. It's where you bring someone into your business to dig into your sales, marketing, and customer performance data to see how well it's all working and where you need to focus your efforts.

I know I often feel like one of the horsemen of the apocalypse, because the news I bring is rarely positive. It's often disheartening.

However, when you're staring at your sales, marketing, and customer performance data for the first time, realising it's not great news, it can be highly motivating. You can choose to see it for what it is: a wake-up call and an opportunity for improvement. Your data always presents you with an opportunity to do better.

A colleague of mine always says that feedback is the breakfast of champions. With data, you get to be the champion who's striving for excellence and marketing mastery.

Doesn't that sound more heroic than avoiding inconvenient truths?

Thoughts and Action Planning

1. How committed are you to business development effectiveness? If it's not your thing, delegate its leadership to someone who cares.

2. Do you have the skills internally to access, analyse, interpret, and act upon your information?

3. Who is your best in-house data slinger?

4. Who's your best database or MS Excel resource?

5. Do you have any design, writing, or programming skills in-house?

6. Who's managing your promotions? Are they running any A/B splits or testing any landing pages on your website?

7. Is there anyone on your leadership team who could serve as your chief information officer?

8. If you lack the internal resources, who else could you rely upon to help get you over the data analysis hurdle?

Resources for Being Effective

Who Moved My Cheese?
by Spencer Johnson, M.D.

The Fifth Discipline
The Art and Practice of the Learning Organization
by Peter M. Senge

Landing Page Optimization
The Definitive Guide to Testing and Tuning for Conversions
by Tim Ash

Managing Customer Experience and Relationships
A Strategic Framework
by Don Peppers and Martha Rogers

Making Sustainability Stick
The Blueprint for Successful Implementation
by Kevin Wilhelm

—— BEING ——
SCALABLE

Preparing for Growth

"We accomplish all that we do through delegation."
Stephen R. Covey

THE BUILD STAGE

BEING SCALABLE

About Being Scalable

Before you can market your business effectively, you need to know how much business you can handle. How much new business can you handle without sacrificing quality or your client's experience?

Being scalable is about increasing your production capacity by increasing some combination of your speed, efficiency, quality, reliability, and consistency of production.

Let's define your production as to how you deliver your client's experience from the first impression to a long-term relationship. This includes how you market and sell, how you serve your clients, how transactions are processed, including the post-sale interactions that drive repeat business.

Because of your efforts to be buyable and systematic, you're already working on aspects of scalability. The first step is to close gaps in your processes and clean up pinch points in your workflows.

If you need inspiration for becoming scalable, consider how, in 1913, Henry Ford transformed his manual process for assembling Model T cars from a 12-hour process down to a 150-minute process. Next, he refined his process further until he could produce a Model T every 24 seconds, which is incredible!

Don't be concerned if you're not a manufacturer and can't streamline to this extent; that is not the goal. Your goal is to maximise how many people you can serve, minimise your effort and costs, and improve the consistency, reliability, and quality of your client and team's experience.

Why Is Being Scalable Necessary?

At a personal level, you scale your business to escape the physical grind and emotional bondage of entrepreneurship.

At a business level, you scale if you want to please your clients, profit from your business, and transform your role from the chief cook and bottle washer to business owner.

You scale if you want your business to grow beyond yourself, stay competitive and, when the time comes, sell your business.

The Costs of Not Being Scalable

The costs of not scaling are high. The most personal of these costs are your time, health, income, and freedom. If you don't scale, you can become tied to your business in a way that is unhealthy and unsustainable.

At a customer level, what you sacrifice is your reputation as you struggle to deliver results consistent with client expectations.

At a team level, you make it challenging and costly to recruit, train, and retain people.

At a financial level, you don't earn what you could from your business, if you were to get it together.

How to Practise Being Scalable

There is no one-size-fits-all approach. You need to work from base principles to build systems that make sense for your situation.

If you're a single person start-up, the first step in being scalable is often as simple as hiring an assistant or a part-time bookkeeper.

The process is to break up your many roles into distinct functions or jobs for someone else to do at a lower cost, with greater focus, speed and quality.

You start by identifying the tasks you hate, that bog you down and keep you from working on higher-value activities and functions.

Typically, you start with the most repetitive tasks, which are the easiest to delegate. For you to effectively delegate these tasks, you need to define your goals, inputs, processes, systems involved, outputs, your time, and customer experience expectations. You need to be systematic.

Once a role is systematised and delegated, you can evaluate its effectiveness. You now have a workflow that can be continually improved over time with some combination of people, machinery, computers and such.

Step by step, you work through each facet of your business from high frequency, high urgency, high importance, to high leverage and on down the list.

Don't constrain this thinking to your back office or the so-called production side of your business. You want to focus on anything effecting your clients or your team's experience, which is everything.

The Call to Action

Don't over-complicate this exercise. It is easy to imagine some assembly line and think, "we're not a factory" and abandon the effort.

Regardless of what you do, I guarantee you there are things you can delegate, roles to create, and aspects of your business you can template and improve if you focus on it.

Is There a Larger Opportunity?

Beyond just splitting up roles and automating tasks, is there an opportunity to transform your business and the opportunity to scale?

How might you take advantage of new technologies to scale your business in ways you never imagined?

The primary difference between investing in incremental improvements and re-imagining your business, is a willingness to explore possibilities.

Are you open to re-imagining your business as something special, disruptive, or counter-intuitive?

If your goal is to scale, completely re-imagining your business might lead to far greater scalability than systematising your existing business model. It's something to think about.

Thoughts and Action Planning

1. What is the one task you do all the time, that you hate and would be thrilled to delegate?

2. Which roles do you enjoy the most, that you are great at, which earn you the most money?

3. What are the lowest value roles you play, and that you routinely spend time on?

4. What are the most frequently occurring and time-consuming tasks in your business?

5. Look to your customer journey map. Where are the bottlenecks that need attention?

6. Make a list of your procedures along your customer's journey as well as all your administrative ones. Now prioritise them in terms of frequency, the expertise required, their importance, and how much time each requires.

7. What is the opportunity in each? Do you need to document and refine the process, invest in systems, or hire some help?

8. What solution will be the fastest to implement, the most scalable, the lowest cost or the lowest risk? Which factors are most important in each situation?

Resources for Being Scalable

The eMyth Revisited
Why Most Small Businesses Don't Work and What to Do About it
by Michael Gerber

Scaling Up
How A Few Companies Make It...And Why The Rest Don't
by Verne Harnish

Traction
Get A Grip on Your Business
by Gino Wickman

Process Mapping, Process Improvement, and Process Management
A Practical Guide to Enhancing Work and Information Flow
by Dan Madison

THE
GROW STAGE

Developing Relationships

THE GROW STAGE

The Ways of Being in the grow stage are about cultivating, nurturing, and developing fruitful relationships.

The grow stage is often problematic. It's highly dependent upon the design and build stages as they set the stage for success or failure.

The grow stage is typically very costly, very high risk, and very public. It is also the most fun and exciting stage. It's where you're out in public, visible, connecting with people, making sales and, ideally, driving earnings growth.

When everything is working, the grow stage is where you reap all the rewards of your design and build efforts. When it is not going well, it's where you rack up substantial losses and risk your reputation.

The Grow Stage Is About Relationship Development:

Being Accessible – showing up where people look

Being Connected – growing your network

Being Endorsed – building your reputation

Being Present – attending to relationships

Being Conspicuous – attracting desired attention

Depending on your business model, you may not need to practise all five Ways. Many businesses rely on one or two Ways to drive all the business they need. The key is to determine which Ways make the most sense for your business and to focus on making those Ways work for you.

—— BEING ——
ACCESSIBLE

Showing Up Where People Look

"To stay on the map, you've got to keep showing up."
Peter Gallagher

THE GROW STAGE

BEING ACCESSIBLE

About Being Accessible

How hard is your business to find? If a prospective client were to go looking for a provider like you, would they find you? What lengths will people need to go to before they find you?

In an age where "going online" to find who and what you need is an instinctual response, you'll either be found, or you'll miss the opportunity entirely.

Sure, people ask their friends for referrals, and you can get business that way. You can also pay to advertise and make yourself known in a variety of other time-consuming and costly manners. But why would you purposefully pay more for business development?

Why would you ignore the easiest, lowest cost, least time-consuming ways to attract people who are actively seeking what you offer? The only solid reasons are:

1. You serve a very exclusive audience
2. Your clients and their friends don't use the Internet
3. Your business is a secret
4. You don't want to

Otherwise, it makes no sense to ignore the low-hanging fruit.

Why Is Being Accessible Necessary?

Being accessible is necessary because you want to be found easily when your ideal clients are seeking help.

1. You want your phone to ring with eager clients on the line
2. You want the business
3. You don't want your competitors to spend less and get more sales

Being found is often the lowest cost sale, requiring the least effort to generate next to sales with existing clients and warm referrals. Do I need to say more?

The only downside of being accessible is that you'll have to deal with a wide variety of inquiries. It can be time-consuming, and you may need a means of lead scoring and pre-qualifying to manage the time involved.

The Costs of Not Being Accessible

Without belabouring the point, the costs of not being easy to find are either obscurity or reliance on costlier business development alternatives.

It is like ignoring the easy-to-reach apples in favour of the ones way out of reach at the top of the tree. Sure, you can drag out the ladder, but why would you?

How to Practise Being Accessible

Being accessible starts with who you want to be accessible to. You need to know your audience well and understand where and how they seek help. The easiest way to gauge demand is to access demand statistics online.

You start by learning how people seek help and the language they use to find things. You want to learn about keywords, hashtags, and categories.

Categories are old school, but still relevant. Think back to the big yellow phone book we used to use, and you'll understand categorical searches. If I want a pizza, I look up pizza in the directory. If I want a marketing consultant, I look up marketing consultants. Online directories are still largely organised by category. You need to know which categories best describe your business and make sure you are included in the listings.

#Hashtags are the new kids on the block. They represent topics of interest, and they can be quite dynamic. Because tags change and trend daily, you'll want to start by targeting the stable, so-called evergreen tags and deal with trends as they emerge.

Twitter, Instagram, Facebook and most of the social media sites are hashtag based.

Keywords are the middle child. Keywords and how to use them is a large topic on its own. Keywords are used wherever people can search for what they want, such as on a search engine or with a website search bar.

160

The idea is simple. You type in what you think you want and the search engine tries to deliver the most relevant items in return.

The variety of terms people use, and their relative frequency of occurrence, define the online demand for what you sell.

The practice is called keyword research, and it's an art and a science that requires empathy, language, and lateral thinking skills to master.

Fortunately, Google and others offer tools for you to understand how people search for what you offer.

The combination of knowing your categories, #hashtags and keywords, and their frequency of occurrence, is the first step in becoming accessible.

Next, you need to determine which sites your target audience uses to search for things and determine if you can afford to compete on those platforms.

A good example of this is the question: "How do I get onto the first page of Google on relevant search terms?" You've likely heard people talk about SEO (search engine optimisation) and SEM (search engine marketing). It's a big deal and a huge opportunity to be among the top listings because the level of exposure can be enormous.

But Google is not the only game in town and what's more important than Google is the idea of being accessible.

There are many ways to be accessible. Rather than defaulting to Google search engine results and competing in what has become a highly competitive arena, you may decide to take an easier path.

You may decide to focus on Google, Bing, and Apple business pages.

You may develop profiles on Facebook, LinkedIn, Instagram, Twitter, Alignable, Pinterest, Meetup and similar social media sites.

You may also make use of marketplaces like eBay, Amazon, Kijiji, AliExpress and sites like them to be accessible.

You can set up listings on directories like Online Yellow Pages, Better Business Bureau (BBB), your local industry association, Manta and similar.

There are also review sites like Yelp, TrustedPros for contractors, the BBB again, TripAdvisor and so on. There are many of these review sites, and they are often industry specific.

The point is not to try to be everywhere. The point is to determine where your prospective clients seek help and to make sure you're visible where they go looking.

You want to be accessible before you start spending money on higher-cost forms of advertising.

Don't forget that simply having a listing and being found is not enough; you still need to be relevant, compelling and easy to buy from to make the most of your accessibility.

The Call to Action

Get clear on which categories, #hashtags and keywords your clients are using, and which sites can help you connect to your niche market.

See if the sites offer a media kit or have tools to help you confirm the site serves your target audience. Next, determine what it will cost for you to be there.

Now, develop a series of short descriptions like an elevator speech to serve as compelling introductions. You'll want to incorporate your target keywords, #hashtags and categories into your introductions to help you connect with prospective clients.

Thoughts and Action Planning

1. Which keywords are your customers most likely to search for solutions with?

2. Which search engines, directories, and online stores do people routinely use to buy similar products or to find what you offer? Are you present on these platforms?

3. Do you have an effective introduction or elevator speech on top directories, that highlights who you are, what you offer, and whom you serve in a keyword-relevant way?

4. If you conduct a keyword, category, or hashtag search on these websites, are you anywhere to be found?

5. Visit your website, and all your social media and directory listings, and cut and paste your introduction copy into a document. How different are the passages? Do any of them serve as an effective introduction?

6. If you're invisible, update your listings with an effective introduction and consider paying for placement, until your listings start to show up in organic searches.

7. Keep things simple to start with. Your goal is to be everywhere your clients go to look for you with a powerful and compelling introduction.

Resources for Being Accessible

Keyword Research
How To Find and Profit From Low Competition Long Tail Keywords
by Nathan George

SEO Fitness Workbook
The Seven Steps to Search Engine Optimization
by Jason McDonald

Web Resources

Ahrefs.com – SEO Tools and Resources

SEMrush.com – Research tools for SEO and SEM

BuzzSumo.com – Content marketing research and monitoring

MyPresences.com – Tool for Managing Local Search Profiles

Search.Google.com - Google Search Console

Bing.com/toolbox/webmaster – Bing Webmaster Tools

—— BEING ——
CONNECTED

Growing Your Network

"If your business comes from relationships, relationships should be your business."

Doug Ales

THE GROW STAGE

BEING CONNECTED

About Being Connected

There's an old saying, "it's not what you know, but who you know" that speaks to the need to be connected.

Bob Burg, an authority on influence and referral marketing, said: "… all things being equal, people will do business with, and refer business to, those people they know, like, and trust".

This discussion is about becoming known, liked, and trusted by the well connected. It's important to build connectivity with the hubs and authorities in your client's community.

Why Is Being Connected Necessary?

Although it takes time to earn the trust of people, your network can be one of the most economical and cost-effective ways to grow your business.

Why? Because you're borrowing trust from the person doing the referring. The more credible and trustworthy the referrer, the more weight the referral has with a potential customer.

With a referral, you are not starting cold with zero trust. Whoever referred you is vouching for you, confirming you are worthy of trust. The idea being, if you trust me, you should trust my recommendation.

This is a huge time saver for everyone involved. The referred person is more apt to proceed on the strength of the existing relationship.

By leveraging your relationships, you can reduce the time, cost and effort involved in earning the trust of others.

The Costs of Not Being Connected

When you're not well connected, you must do all the heavy lifting of earning trust and developing relationships. You need to show up and put the time in to earn people's trust from scratch.

If you're comfortable with direct selling, no problem, it's part of the job. You can become efficient and systematic about it.

If you're a solopreneur, small business owner, or executive, you may struggle to find the time to network, or cultivate and nurture relationships regularly.

However, if you don't take the time, you'll put yourself at a disadvantage to your better-connected peers.

Without strategic relationships, your access to prime opportunities will be limited. You'll need to rely more on advertising and promotional efforts to compensate for your lack of connectivity.

All this extra effort and expense makes you less competitive and potentially less profitable.

How to Practise Being Connected

Without getting too deep into networking theory, there are three types of people in a network. There are authorities, hubs, and nodes.

Authorities are experts in their field. People know them as the "go-to" people with all the answers. They know other experts and leaders in their field. They are characterised as having high connectivity.

Hubs are, by definition, popular within their industry. They are not necessarily experts, but due to their position, everyone knows them. Social media influencers, journalists, and salespeople are hubs because of their visibility and the sheer number of people they interact with.

Nodes are everyone else. Nodes are characterised as having low connectivity. They are neither popular nor experts in their fields.

When your goal is to become more connected within your industry or niche market, the fastest way to increase your connectivity is to become known by the hubs and authorities in your client's community.

Once you are known, liked, and trusted by a few hubs and authorities, they start vouching for you, and you'll see more lead volume. Their referrals will tend to be better qualified, and you'll find the leads faster and easier to close than you would with cold leads from advertising.

The Call to Action

To increase your connectivity, you'll want to look at your target market as a community with many facets. Imagine an orange cut across the middle. Visualise the triangular wedges radiating out from the centre.

Each wedge is a facet of your client's community with hubs and authorities of its own.

For example, colleges and universities, government regulators, key manufacturers, industry associations, and key suppliers belong to different wedges or facets of the community.

Your goal is to get to know the hubs and authorities in each wedge. Figure out who you like, relate to, and have the potential to develop a win/win relationship with. You want to find people who serve the same target audience as you, who share your values and intentions.

Being connected is not just about knowing people; it is about fostering legitimate relationships with people with mutual interest and intent to serve your target market.

Over time, your goal is to foster relationships with well-aligned hubs and authorities, in every facet of your client's community.

If you believe in the idea that "the community raises the child", your goal is to mobilise and rally community leaders to your cause. It's not about being a social butterfly. It is about stepping up as a leader and enrolling people in the possibility you represent. You want people to understand the role you play in serving their community, so they can help you serve.

You can't serve a whole community on your own. You need to find like-minded leaders and rally them around your mission. To do this, you first need to know who the community leaders are, and they need to know who you are.

Make a list of your target hubs and authorities, and prioritise who you need to get to know. Then reach out and ask for an interview. Get to know them and build relationships.

When you make a habit of cultivating and nurturing these sorts of relationships, you'll get more referrals.

Remember it takes time to build authentic relationships.

Your goal is to make it as easy as possible for people to get to know you and to refer you to others.

If you're practising the first nine Ways in the design stage, this will be easier. If you are practising the six Ways of Being in the build stage, it is easier again. Why? Because people will be able to see your level of clarity and commitment. The reasons for them to like, trust, and refer you will be laid out in front of them.

The last step is to make it easy for your community to make introductions.

If you have valuable offers to share with their community, they are more likely to share your offer. If you don't have something specific and tangible for people to share, you'll make it more difficult for people to recommend you.

There is not much point in developing high leverage relationships with the hubs and authorities in a community and then do nothing to mobilise their support.

Consider hosting an event or a seminar. Create a useful app, eBook or a downloadable resource for people to share with their community. Make it easy for your community to understand how you create value in a way that is easily shared.

Thoughts and Action Planning

Think about your different communities:

- family and friends
- professional network
- online networks
- target client's network

You can be well-connected within each of these communities and generate business connections from all of them.

1. Start by defining your client's community. What are the facets of their community? Who are their trusted advisors? What do they buy? What do they read? Do they belong to an association? Draw your client's community. Use a dartboard visual to describe their community. Use the concentric rings and wedges to map out the community structure. Each wedge is a different facet of your client's community. The closer someone is to the inner ring, the greater their connectivity.

2. Who do you know in or near the inner ring? Who would you like them to introduce you to?

3. Which online networks do you need to focus on? Where does your target audience actively participate?

4. What will you do to increase your connectivity?

Resources for Being Connected

Linked

How Everything is Connected to Everything Else and What it Means for Business, Science and Everyday Life

by Albert-Laszlo Barabasi

Beyond Influencer Marketing

Create Connections with Influential People to Build Authority, Grow Your List, and Boost Revenue

by Cloris Kylie

Making Your Net Work

The Art and Science of Career and Business Networking

by Billy Dexter and Melissa G Wilson

Making Connections That Count

The Gimmick-free Guide to Authentic Online Relationships with Influencers and Followers

by Michal Stawicki

— BEING —
ENDORSABLE

Building Your Reputation

"You can't buy a good reputation,
you must earn it."

Harvey Mackay

THE GROW STAGE

BEING ENDORSABLE

About Being Endorsable

Ken Blanchard, the author of over 60 business books including the *One Minute Manager*, said "None of us is as smart as all of us" and that's the benefit of crowd-based endorsements. We get to learn from each other's experiences.

The law defines testimonials as given by regular people, and endorsements as given by celebrities for money but, generally, the law treats them according to the same set of rules. The rules state that testimonials must be legitimate, truthful, and not misleading or deceptive.

I'm going to stay out of the legal conversation and stick with the intentionality behind why you want people to share their honest opinion or experience with others. I'm also going to use the terms testimonial and endorsement interchangeably.

I will say it's important to understand the law as it pertains to testimonials and endorsements, so you don't inadvertently stumble into trouble.

On the surface, endorsements and testimonials can seem a bit like referrals, but referrals are an extension of trust, whereas testimonials come from a desire to share.

Good or bad, if you've had a strong emotional experience, you're likely to share it with others. You'll invite people to learn from your experience because sharing increases your recognition and social status.

Endorsements come in many forms; from verbal sharing to online social posts, social media likes and shares, article reviews, blog posts, client testimonials, expert and celebrity endorsements, news media stories, and industry awards.

Whatever the form, endorsements serve to create awareness and transfer approval from one person or organisation to another. They transfer knowledge, energy, credibility, value, and the implied values associated with the one doing the endorsing.

Endorsements are a powerful social lubricant to help overcome resistance and scepticism.

Why Is Being Endorsed Necessary?

Cultivating reviews and endorsements is an important aspect of your marketing mix. This is because people are more inclined to believe what others say about you than what you say about yourself.

Beyond the facts that get shared, endorsements convey a complex mix of emotions. This is especially true of audio and video testimonials. Emotions are where most decisions are made. We need to feel our way into decisions, and endorsements guide our feelings one way or the other.

Endorsements are often story based as well. When someone shares their personal experience, they tell you a short story about what they did and why, how it all went down, how they feel about it, and whether they think you should do it too. Personal stories are powerful. It's a wonderful win/win/win scenario.

The Costs of Not Being Endorsed

The alternative to being endorsed are costly investments in sales and advertising. Without endorsements, your sales cycle times slow considerably.

Without endorsements, people have nothing but your word to go by. In simplest terms, cultivating forms of social endorsement save you time and money.

How to Practise Being Endorsed

Practising being endorsable has two basic requirements.

The first and most important requirement is to be worthy of endorsement by your target audience. What does that mean?

Being worthy means that people will not share their opinion unless you are worthy of it. Put another way, people will share whatever opinion you are worthy of. If you disappointed them, you are worthy of a negative review.

While you can't please everyone all the time, you should be able to please your target audience most of the time, or you will accumulate negative reviews.

Your operational excellence, quality, and customer service experience are central to receiving positive reviews and shares.

However, if you want to encourage the sharing behaviour, you need to make it easy for people to endorse you publicly. Ask your clients to share their experience. Tell them what you would like them to do.

The easiest way to support would-be reviewers is to make everything they need readily available, along with instructions and guidelines to follow.

If you're seeking endorsements from the media, social influencers and bloggers, you want to anticipate their needs. Gather up your storytelling resources and put them on your website as a press kit or media kit.

Your media kit includes product and contextual photos, videos, logos, and key messaging for your products and services. It should also include information about you and your company.

If you have quotes and testimonials, share them. If you have third party studies, share them. If you've won any awards or received industry recognition, share those too.

Provide contact information for a person who can help with ordering samples, trials, and scheduling interviews.

You'll want to answer the standard who, what, when, where, why and how questions that help other people tell your story. Keep your answers brief and to the point.

Ideally, your media kit will include a well-crafted version of your story, so others can use it to write derivative stories.

Keep in mind no one wants to spend hours finding what they need to tell your story. You want to make it as easy as you can.

The Call to Action

The practice of being endorsable starts and ends with the quality of your products and services, and the experience you create for people.

Beyond that, it is equally important to ask people to share their experience with others and to make it very easy for them to do so.

Depending on your business, there will be different places for people to endorse you. Google reviews, Amazon, Yelp, TripAdvisor, RateMD or HomeStars are common examples.

Start where people shop and encourage clients to share. If there is no obvious option, make it easy for people to share on your website, or with a satisfaction survey.

Thoughts and Action Planning

1. Where are most people likely to see your endorsements?

2. Which sites are more important to your clients: Google My Business, social profiles like LinkedIn or Alignable, review sites like Yelp, or marketplaces like Amazon, eBay or the like?

3. What practices might you put in place to solicit reviews and testimonials?

4. Have you considered using a third party interviewer to gather more insightful information?

5. Have you considered adding a questionnaire or a link to an online survey, on your invoices?

6. Have you considered inviting your top clients to appear in a testimonial video?

Resources for Being Endorsed

Referrals And...

Recommendations, Introductions, Endorsements, Testimonials, Reviews and Word of Mouth

by Dean Willeford

Authority Marketing

How to Leverage 7 Pillars of Thought Leadership to Make Competition Irrelevant

by Adam Witty and Rusty Shelton

The New Rules of Marketing and PR

How to Use Social Media, Online Video, Mobile Applications, Blogs, News Jacking, and Viral Marketing to Reach Buyers Directly

by David Meerman Scott

Spark

The Complete Public Relations Guide for Small Business

by Robert Deigh

PRESENT

Attending To Relationships

"The simple act of paying attention
can take you a long way."
Keanu Reeves

THE GROW STAGE

BEING PRESENT

About Being Present

How much do you appreciate it when someone shows a legitimate interest in you? How about when they listen carefully to what you say and ask insightful questions that show they're "listening into" what you've said?

What if someone picks up on your non-verbal clues and anticipates your needs? What would you think of someone who shows you appreciation by acknowledging you in ways they know you'll appreciate?

No, I'm not talking about some character in a W-Network movie. I'm talking about the things relationships are built upon, that are universally appreciated.

Being present is a gift we give to people, and it is an exceptional and cost-effective way to start and nurture your business relationships. It is also very hard for your competitors to replicate.

No, it's not creepy, and it's more than good manners. If your business is all about relationships, being present is a very cost-effective way to be the kind of person or company that people tell their friends and colleagues about and refer people to.

Think about it. When you can't go out for dinner with your family without everyone's attention locked on their smartphones, how much will people appreciate your presence?

How about when you recognise people for their contributions and efforts with attention and acknowledgement? Does that enhance a relationship?

How about well-timed gestures and invitations to do things together? Same thing, right? It helps to deepen the bond.

Be honest, how well-practised and consistent are you with these behaviours with your best clients, industry peers, or your spouse or partner for that matter?

Why Is Being Present Necessary?

When you fully appreciate how much business is about fostering and developing mutually beneficial relationships, it becomes clear that you need to develop your relationship building routines and practices.

Unfortunately, outside of kindergarten, we don't get much by way of relationship training. Your technique might be poorly developed. Practical incompetence in relationship development can greatly limit your earnings and growth potential.

I know I started with a low level of competence in this area. I was doing almost everything wrong that I could do wrong. It was not from a place of ego or malice; I simply did not know how ineffective my practices were until my coach pointed it out so many years ago.

With insightful suggestions, he encouraged me down a learning path I'm still working on today.

Once I got past the basic training about how to actively listen, negotiate, and manage my emotional triggers, I started to understand that being present to another person is central to being in a relationship. But what does being present mean?

In the James Cameron movie Avatar, there is a Navii greeting, "I see you", which is explained as meaning "I see into you". Which translates roughly into "I am present to who you are".

Is that not what you wanted from your parents as a child? Did you not long for them to see you and appreciate you for who you were? It's a very powerful gift to be present to someone. It can feel uncomfortable at first because it is so unfamiliar. However, once you overcome your discomfort, people generally have the experience of feeling heard and understood.

The experience is intimate, and it provides the foundation upon which you can build meaningful relationships.

The sad thing is, being distracted by your smartphone, task-focused, and oblivious to who the people are around you is pretty much the opposite of this Way of Being.

It is this fully present, attentive, gracious, respectful Way of Being that earns us our best relationships.

The Costs of Not Being Present

If your focus is always internal or task-focused, you miss the opportunity to know and be known. You build superficial relationships that do not last, and that foster no loyalty or empathy. As a result, you do not realise the potential value of any client relationship. You and your clients remain transactional, which renders you easily replaceable by competitors.

How to Practise Being Present

There are many facets to being present.

The first one is safety. You need to create a safe place where people can be authentic and share what is real for them. Turn your ringer off and put away your cell phone while you are with someone as a show of respect.

The more you sit in your self-importance, the less safe you make it for people to share. Park your agenda long enough to listen to what people are saying and you'll learn something about them.

Don't try to correct or be right; just listen and hear what people are saying. Actively paraphrase what you heard, then respond with insightful questions to show them you were listening thoughtfully.

Accept what people say by showing compassion to, and acceptance of, their feelings. Stay out of your judging and critical headspace long enough to hear what is being said from their perspective. Make sure to maintain eye contact without being intimidating.

This is not about giving people the space to vent. It is about learning to lead conversations where the other person is doing most of the talking, and you are enabling them to be real with you and to share.

In the time it takes to make someone feel safe, heard, valued, and respected, you will have laid some big relationship paving stones. You'll have earned trust and appreciation for creating a safe place to be heard.

These moments are endearing. They invite the other person to return the favour and to hear you as well.

Over time, these experiences accumulate and the next thing you know your client is a friend, and you are a trusted confidant and advisor.

So how does that work en masse? What if your contact list is too large for meaningful one-to-one interactions?

You can still treat people with respect and acknowledge what they mean to you and your business. You'll need to maintain a database where you manage your relationships, beyond simply recording contact information.

With a database, you can send personalised offers, thank you notes, referrals, recommendations, best wishes, congratulations, acknowledgement, invitations, and gifts of gratitude that demonstrate you care enough to be present to the relationship.

What's important is your actions are authentic. People pick up on inauthentic gestures as they demonstrate you are motivated by self-interest rather than mutual gain. These self-serving gestures can backfire and sour relationships. You need to think through your acknowledgement and recognition efforts carefully.

The Call to Action

Stop trying to sell all the time. Make it your goal to be genuinely interested and friendly. Learn who the person, sitting across from you, is. Don't let your desire to sell take you off track.

I'm not suggesting you engage in endless small talk. You need to take charge of the conversation and be productive with it.

Make sure you capture the essence of what you've learned in your client database. This allows you to remember important details so you can initiate follow-up and pick up where you left off in the conversation. Initiative and recall are important as they show you were listening and that you are invested in the relationship.

You may be a careful listener and have a decent memory, but we all have limits. You can't reasonably expect to remember the little details from hundreds of conversations without some system to help you.

Don't mistake these meetings for a counselling session; this is still business. Yes, you are building relationships, but you are also listening carefully to what is not being said.

Active listening affords you some control over the conversation as you can ask pointed questions that serve you both and set you up for a mutually successful business relationship full of new opportunities.

Thoughts and Action Planning

1. How do you show up in meetings with prospects and clients? Are you present to them and the relationship, or are you fixated on pitching?

2. Do you maintain a customer database where you track information in addition to contact and transactional details?

3. Have you categorised your database with relationship stages like prospect, client, repeat client, volunteer, media, advocate, and influencer? Do you record whether people give you referrals or whether to send them a gift during the holidays?

4. Do you know what people like so you can invite them out to events or share something they'll find interesting and appreciate?

5. Do you have a schedule where you regularly reach out to people?

6. Do you have an account with a florist or gift designer to make it easy to recognise people for their efforts or their contribution to your business?

The challenge in being present to relationships is the time it takes. You need to make managing relationships easy and systematic, or you will not do it.

Resources for Being Present

Leader Effectiveness Training: L.E.T.
by Thomas Gordon

How to Win Friends and Influence People
by Dale Carnegie

The Customer Centricity Playbook
Implementing a Winning Strategy Driven by Customer Lifetime Value
by Peter Fader and Sarah E Toms

Keep Your Donors
The Better Guide to Better Communication & Stronger Relationships
by Tom Ahern and Simone P. Joyaux

The Art of Community
Seven Principles for Belonging
by Charles Vogl

The Art of Community
Building the New Age of Participation
by Jono Bacon

BEING
CONSPICUOUS

Attracting Desired Attention

"Be so good they can't ignore you."
Steve Martin

THE GROW STAGE

BEING CONSPICUOUS

About Being Conspicuous

The final Way in this program is being conspicuous.

Conspicuous has a simple meaning which is to stand out, to be highly visible, obvious, or attention-getting.

Standing out and getting attention is desirable, beneficial, and a worthy goal provided the attention you generate is purposeful and well received.

Being conspicuous with advertising, sponsorships, out of door advertising, and public relations (PR) can be very powerful. However, it is highly risky at the same time. You need to be well prepared if you're to have any chance of earning a return on your investment.

Have you ever been subjected to a beginner violinist, or new bagpiper, practising loudly? Did the sound make your skin crawl, and erode your patience to the point where you just needed to escape the noise?

Have you ever been in a retail store, where they're playing good music, but there is so much static and noise from their worn-out speakers, it grates on your nerves? You try not to listen, but you find yourself compelled to move away from the assault on your ears.

The so-called music is highly conspicuous, but the result served only to drive you away.

If you want people to appreciate your music, you start by learning to play an instrument. Then before you perform, you quietly tune your instrument and warm up before amplifying the sound. Ideally, your amplifier and speakers are in good order. Then if your music resonates, you will "Pied Piper" people into your business.

Consider your promotions and advertising in the same context.

By simply amplifying your unpractised, ill tuned, and unrefined message with advertising, you're more likely to assault your audience's senses than you are to draw them in.

Now consider all the free publicity US President Donald Trump gets from the media. The man is as conspicuous as you can be, but the coverage is so negative, it erodes his brand.

There's a good reason being conspicuous is the twentieth Way of Being and not the first, as many wish it were.

The reason is simple. You need to be ready (in tune and know how to play) before you amplify your message. If you're not prepared, you risk driving people away, damaging your brand, and wasting money in the process.

Why Is Being Conspicuous Necessary?

Being conspicuous is not always necessary. Many businesses get along just fine without it. They do so because they are successfully practising the other Ways of Being, and they have enough business without advertising.

That said, if you have a high volume, transactional business, being conspicuous may be your only choice.

Why? Because of the sheer numbers of people you need to reach. Sometimes public relations and mass marketing are the only cost-effective option to drive awareness and create brand preference at the scale you operate.

There is no right answer, only an approach that makes sense to your business. What's important is that you understand your goals, needs, options, and economics. Once you're clear, you can make conscious choices about how to be conspicuous to your target audience.

The Costs of Not Being Conspicuous

Assuming Being Conspicuous is right for you; the cost of not being highly visible and obvious is obscurity and insufficient sales, and that will not do.

If you have something wonderful to offer, you need to get it out there so people can enjoy it and your business can prosper.

How to Practise Being Conspicuous

Your first step is to reference your work from previous chapters. If you are to be attractively conspicuous, you need to have your act together.

You need to be recognisable, relevant, attractive, affective, compelling, informed, systematic, effective, and scalable.

If you're still weak in these nine areas, you're unlikely to be successful in your advertising or public relations efforts.

If you are ready, do you focus on public relations, advertising, signage, sponsorships, shows, events, or some combination?

What mix is going to provide the targeting, reach, frequency, engagement, and response rates to justify your investment?

You'll want to develop a proforma model to gauge your risk and return with different scenarios to help you understand your options.

Once you've selected your mix of promotional channels, you'll need to develop and allocate funds to each channel. Once you know what you can invest, you can plan the campaign and move to implement.

You'll want to consider each channel as part of an integrated multi-channel whole, like a band compared to a soloist.

Being conspicuous is a very high-cost, high-risk, and fast-paced arena. You'll want to track the performance of each channel and segment in near to real-time so you can adjust your approach quickly and actively.

Ideally, you want to think of your advertising as if it were an investment portfolio. You want consolidated reporting to understand the performance of the whole portfolio. You also want to be able to drill down into the individual equities to monitor their performance.

Advertising is moving ever closer to behaving like an actively managed, day trading portfolio. With advertising, a buy and hold strategy is not what you want. Those days are gone.

If you're dealing with media suppliers and no one is talking about A/B splits and multivariate testing, ROI or active campaign management, you need to find some other people to speak with.

The larger and more complex your campaign, the greater the opportunity for rapid iteration and testing.

Don't make the mistake of blowing your budget on the perfect campaign. Anticipate an iterative (design, deploy, test and redesign) process where you continuously improve performance.

Public relations are another matter entirely. The single most important facet of PR is working with industry insiders who are connected to popular writers and social influencers in your client's world.

It's not impossible to build influencer relationships on your own, but it can be very costly and time-consuming. Be very selective in choosing a public relations provider and make sure you're relevant, attractive, affective, and compelling, on top of all the Ways of Being in the build stage. You need to be prepared for what media coverage can deliver.

Industry and public tradeshows are a different beast as well, with different goals and objectives. Shows can be a huge waste of money or a vital lynchpin for integrating everything else in your business plan.

What's common to every mass media channel is the need to be well-practised and have your act together with the preceding ways before you invest heavily in being conspicuous.

The Call to Action

This may be a reverse call to action, but don't rush into being conspicuous. It is exciting, sexy, high leverage, terribly risky, and challenging to get right.

If you need to jump into it before you're ready, focus on risk mitigation. Set up your campaigns with short timelines, run A/B split tests on your creative, and then segment your audience with different messages.

In this way, you can quickly test what works, and learn who is most responsive. Which devices are most important, and how effortlessly are people moving through your engagement mechanism and sales conversion process?

By running a series of experiments with ever-tightening constraints, you will manage your risks, learn rapidly, and maximise your results.

The challenge is finding suppliers who will work with you in this manner. This approach is best for you, not necessarily the easiest way for suppliers. This Way creates accountability and results, while the alternative empties your wallet.

Thoughts and Action Planning

1. Do you need to be highly conspicuous? Is advertising essential to your business?

2. Are you prepared for the volume of business that successful advertising can bring?

3. Are you clear on your promotional objectives? What are your time urgent offers and your calls to action?

4. What are your target and breakeven conversion rates?

5. Which media allows you to target most effectively?

6. Which media allow you to buy in test quantities and supports design iterations?

7. What is your media mix?

8. How will you track your advertising investments?

9. How will you refine your media buy, based on the performance feedback you receive?

Resources for Being Conspicuous

I offer several free eBooks on my website to help you frame your thinking. Download them at AccrueMarketing.com. The two listed here are the most relevant to this Way of Being.

Making The Shift
From Random Acts of Marketing to Earnings Growth
by John H. Watson

Investing In Advertising?
Or Hoping For A Big Win
by John H. Watson

More comprehensive titles to read:
Media Planning & Buying
In The 21ST Century
by Ronald Geskey

The Media Handbook
A Complete Guide to Advertising Media Selection, Planning, Research, and Buying
by Helen Katz

Inbound Marketing
Attract, Engage, and Delight Customers Online
by Brian Halligan and Dharmesh Shah

THE
WRAP UP

Using the Ways of Being

USING THE WAYS OF BEING

Admittedly, Ways of Being is a novel way of looking at marketing. It is much easier to go with the flow and focus on tactics versus cultivating and managing your Ways of Being.

However, what you risk is getting caught up in tactics and losing sight of why; what's the purpose of each tactic? How will it contribute to easing your client's purchase process, improving your competitiveness and your bottom line? How will you ensure you're not getting lost in random acts of marketing?

The First Challenge to Overcome

As I've developed and used the Ways of Being in my own business and consulting practice, my biggest challenge has been confusion. If I start talking Ways of Being, people don't know what the heck I'm talking about.

Ways are not part of a marketer's vocabulary. I've found few people are prepared to have why conversations at all. People expect you to know why, so they can focus on how.

My suggestion is to keep the Ways of Being conversation within your leadership and performance measurement teams.

I'm not suggesting you keep the Ways from the rest of your team. They will benefit if they are interested. The point is, the Ways are not really for them. It's a planning and diagnostic framework to help you decide where to invest and in what order.

The people who generally use a map are the driver and the navigator. You don't need everyone's input into where you're going and how to get there. That's your job. What you need is for people to help you implement your plan. You don't need to confuse them with the Ways.

How Does That Work?

Use the Ways as a strategic planning and organising tool. When you're developing your marketing plan, budgets, and rollout sequences, use the Ways to think through your needs.

Look at your system or the system you want to build and ask yourself: Where are the gaps? If there's a performance issue, look to the Ways to help you isolate problems.

When you're developing your marketing plan, pull out the Ways map. Start at the beginning and ask yourself: Where are we?

Where are we weak, where are the gaps in our system? How do we compensate?

Start from the earliest Ways and work your way forward. The greatest leverage comes from strengthening your foundation.

Once you've identified gaps and opportunities, start fitting your tactics, projects, and campaigns into the Ways they serve. The Ways map provides a natural order of operations.

It's an Asset Allocation Exercise

Think about an investment portfolio. The Ways of Being are like asset classes. When you're developing a system for business development, you want to allocate resources to the asset classes that make the most sense in your portfolio.

Your asset allocation should change over time to reflect your progress and needs. In an early-stage company, the asset mix will favour Ways in the design and build stages. As you pull your system together, your asset allocation should weigh more heavily towards the Ways in the growth stage. You're always rebalancing your asset allocation into a mix that makes sense.

The Systems View of Marketing

Once you start to see marketing from this elevated, big-picture vantage point, you'll see your system at work. Once you see the system, you can measure performance along its length, and highlight where to focus your attention.

Part of the asset allocation exercise is to ensure sufficient resources are allocated to continuous performance improvements. This is how the Ways serve you in a diagnostic sense.

By keeping all the Ways in context, you can manage marketing more holistically and systematically. You can allocate resources to tracking, diagnostics, testing, and performance improvements along the length of your client development process.

Tactics Are Vital

Your marketing implementation team will want to focus on tactics and may get confused by the Ways language. Don't force it on them.

The Ways are meant for marketing leaders and navigators to help organise and optimise investments.

Once you've used the Ways for planning and direction, you can go back to your team with a tactical sequence they will understand and run with.

Then, as the leader of your marketing program, you can introduce the Ways conversations a little at a time. You can explain the reasons why the rollout sequence is what it is.

You can create a sense of purpose and direction without bogging people down in a new way of thinking.

Start with why you have chosen each tactic. Define its purpose. Make it clear how you intend to measure success. Then you can bring people into the conversation a little at a time.

I've found as long as I don't fixate on the language of the Ways, I don't confuse people.

Just remember the Ways are for you; to help you see where you're going; for navigating and course-correcting as you move forward.

I know I've been frustrated whenever I've tried to engage writers, programmers, and designers in the Ways conversation. It's not that they can't understand it, but that it takes them time to get over their resistance and get up to speed.

I've learned the hard way that they don't need to know. The Ways are for me, and I can translate my purpose and intentions back into language my suppliers understand.

I encourage you to use the Ways as a strategic tool within your leadership team first.

If you're going to engage your team in a big conversation, start by focusing on your client's journey through your business, or how to maximise lifetime value. Get your team to look at business development systematically first. Once they adopt a systems view, get them familiar with tracking and performance measurement. Once they gain an appreciation for your data, they'll need to learn to act on the data, by running experiments and thinking continuous improvement.

Once you get people thinking and acting differently, the Ways of Being will make far more sense. You'll find your people will get the ideas as a natural next step in a larger marketing conversation.

CLOSING THOUGHTS

The 20 Ways are intended to help you understand and confidently invest in marketing and business development systems.

Being attentive to the 20 Ways will help you take greater ownership over business development by helping you do the right things in the right order to maximise results.

The Ways will help you become more systematic and make you more resistant to being sold on magic bullets and quick fixes.

Beyond this, my personal goal for you is to feel a sense of power and confidence in where you're going, and how you plan to get there.

I'm also hoping these conversations about Ways of Being will spill over into your private life. Specifically, how you approach things like personal leadership, self-mastery, relationships, and parenting.

I've found the Ways of Being to be a powerful construct with far-reaching implications in my own life.

I hope you found these conversations valuable, and I invite you to expand your understanding with the many resources shared in this book and on the Accrue Marketing website.

Visit AccrueMarketing.com/free-marketing-downloads/ and please join us in conversation at AccrueMarketing.com/Blog/

A SIMPLE REQUEST

If you found this book helpful, please share your opinion on Amazon, your favourite book review site, your social profile, or your blog.

Your opinion matters. It helps other business owners make an informed choice of whether this book is right for them.

Your opinion matters to me as well. I'd like to know what you think. No one can see the outside of the box from the inside of the box. I want this book to evolve and become more and more useful. But I can't do that without your feedback.

If you have suggestions, send me an email. Use the contact form on the Accrue Marketing website. It will be directed to me, and I will read it and get back to you.

Thank you in advance for sharing your opinion.

BIBLIOGRAPHY

Ahern, Tom, and Simone P. Joyaux. *Keep Your Donors: The Guide to Better Communications & Stronger Relationships.* John Wiley, 2008.

Albee, Ardath. *EMarketing Strategies for the Complex Sale.* New York: McGraw-Hill, 2010.

Ash, Tim, et al. *Landing Page Optimization: The Definitive Guide to Testing and Tuning for Conversions.* John Wiley & Sons, 2012.

At, Mary Walton, and W. Edwards Deming. *The Deming Management Method.* Chalford: Management Books, 2000, 1996.

Aulet, Bill. *Disciplined Entrepreneurship: 24 Steps to a Successful Startup.* Hoboken, NJ: Wiley, 2015.

Bacon, Jono. *The Art of Community: Building the New Age of Participation.* O'Reilly & Associates, 2012.

Baldridge, Joy J. D. *The Fast Forward MBA in Selling: Become a Self-motivated Profit-center - and Prosper.* New York: Wiley, 2000.

Banks, Drew, and Kim Daus. *Customer.Community: Unleashing the Power of Your Customer Base.* San Francisco: Jossey-Bass, 2002.

Barabási Albert-László. *Linked: How Everything Is Connected to Everything Else and What It Means for Business, Science, and Everyday Life.* Basic Books, a Member of the Perseus Books Group, 2014.

Beckwith, Harry. *Selling the Invisible: A Field Guide to Modern Marketing.* New York: Grand Central Publishing, 2012.

Bly, Robert W. *Business to Business Direct Marketing: Proven Direct Response Methods to Generate More Leaders and Sales.* Lincolnwood, IL: NTC Business Books, 1998.

Breithaupt, Tim. *Take This Job and Love It!: The Joys of Professional Selling.* Calgary: Tim Breithaupt, 1999.

"Buddhism - The Eightfold Path." Buddhism - Rebirth. Accessed December 28, 2017. https://www.buddha101.com/p_path.htm.

Buley, Leah. *The User Experience Team of One: a Research and Design Survival Guide.* Rosenfeld Media, 2013.

Caponi, Todd. *The Transparency Sale: How Unexpected Honesty and Understanding the Buying Brain Can Transform Your Results.* Ideapress Publishing, 2018.

Carnegie, Dale. *How to Win Friends and Influence People.* New-York: Pockets Books, 1936.

Charvet, Shelle Rose. *Words That Change Minds: the 14 Patterns for Mastering the Language of Influence.* Shelle Rose Charvet, 2019.

Ciaramicoli, Arthur P., and Katherine Ketcham. *The Power of Empathy: A Practical Guide to Creating Intimacy, Self-understanding and Lasting Love.* New York: Plume, 2001.

Coe, John M. *The Fundamentals of Business to Business Sales and Marketing.* New York: McGraw-Hill, 2004.

Collins, Jim. *Good to Great: Why Some Companies Make the Leap ... and Others Don't.* London: Random House, 2001.

Collins, Jim, and Jerry I. Porras. *Built to Last: Successful Habits of Visionary Companies.* New York: Harper Business, 2004.

Connor, Richard A., and Jeffrey P. Davidson. Marketing Your Consulting and Professional Services. New York: Wiley, 1997.

Covey, Stephen R. *The Seven Habits of Highly Effective People.* Corby: Institute of Management Foundation, 1998.

Covey, Stephen R. *Principle-Centered Leadership.* Simon & Schuster, 2003.

Covey, Stephen R. *First Things First.* London: Simon & Schuster, 2012.

Covey, Stephen M. R. *The Speed of Trust.* New York: Free Press, 2006.

Curedale, Robert. *Empathy Maps: Step-by-Step Guide.* Design Community College, 2019.

Deigh, Robert. *Spark: the Complete Public Relations Guide for Small Business.* Rdc Public Relations, 2018.

Deming, W. Edwards. *The Essential Deming: Leadership Principles from the Father of Quality.* McGraw-Hill, 2013.

Dexter, Billy, and Melissa G. Wilson. *Making Your Net Work: Mastering the Art and Science of Career and Business Networking.* Networlding Publishing, 2017.

Doerr, John E. *Measure What Matters: OKRs, the Simple Idea That Drives 10x Growth.* Portfolio, 2018.

Duarte, Nancy. Resonate: *Present Visual Stories That Transform Audiences.* Hoboken, NJ: Wiley, 2010.

Eisenberg, Bryan, John Quarto-vonTivadar, and Lisa T. Davis. *Always Be Testing: The Complete Guide to Google Website Optimizer.* Indianapolis: Wiley Publishing, 2008.

Elias, Craig, and Tibor Shanto. *Shift!* IUniverse Inc., 2010.

Enge, Eric, Stephan Spencer, and Jessie C. Stricchiola. *The Art of SEO: Mastering Search Engine Optimization.* Beijing: OReilly, 2015.

Fader, Peter S., and Sarah E. Toms. *The Customer Centricity Playbook: Implement a Winning Strategy Driven by Customer Lifetime Value.* Wharton Digital Press, 2018.

Flinders, Carol L. *The Values of Belonging: Rediscovering Balance, Mutuality, Intuition, and Wholeness in a Competitive World.* New York: HarperCollins E-books, 2010.

George, Nathan. *Keyword Research How To Find and Profit From Low Competition Long Tail Keywords.* Create Space, 2015.

Gerber, Michael E. E-Myth Mastery: *The Seven Essential Disciplines for Building a World Class Company.* New York: HarperCollins E-books, 2009.

Gerber, Michael E. *The e-Myth Revisited: Why Most Small Businesses Don't Work and What to Do About It.* HarperBusiness, 2011.

Geskey, Ronald D. *Media Planning & Buying in the 21st Century.* 2020:Marketing Communications LLC, 2017.

Gordon, Thomas. *Leader Effectiveness Training, L.E.T.: Proven Skills for Leading Today's Business into Tomorrow.* Perigee, 2001.

Gostick, Adrian Robert., and Dana Telford. *The Integrity Advantage.* Salt Lake City: Gibbs Smith, 2004.

Gyatso, Tenzin. *The Art of Happiness: A Handbook for Living.* Sydney: Hodder, 1999.

Halligan, Brian, and Dharmesh Shah. *Inbound Marketing: Get Found Using Google, Social Media, and Blogs.* Hoboken: John Wiley & Sons, 2014.

Harnish, Verne. *Scaling Up: How a Few Companies Make It ... and Why the Rest Don't.* Ashburn, VA: Gazelles, 2015.

Hawkins, David R. *Power vs Force: The Hidden Determinants of Human Behavior.* Carlsbad, CA: Hay House, 2014.

Heath, Chip, and Dan Heath. *Made to Stick: Why Some Ideas Survive and Others Die.* New York: Random House, 2010.

Hopkins, Claude C. *Scientific Advertising,* By Claude Hopkins. Introd. by David Ogilvy. New York, Bell, 1966.

Humberstone, Fiona. *How to Style Your Brand: Everything You Need to Know to Create a Distinctive Brand Identity.* Copper Beech Press, 2016.

Hunt, Ben. *Save the Pixel: The Art of Simple Web Design.* Sheffield: B. Hunt, 2008.

Jantsch, John. *Duct Tape Marketing The World's Most Practical Small Business Marketing Guide.* Nashville: Thomas Nelson, 2011.

Jeffery, Mark. *Data-Driven Marketing: The 15 Metrics Everyone in Marketing Should Know.* Hoboken: Wiley, 2010.

Johnson, Spencer. *Who Moved My Cheese?: An Amazing Way to Deal with Change in Your Work and in Your Life.* Vermilion, 2007.

Katz, Helen. *The Media Handbook a Complete Guide to Advertising Media Selection, Planning, Research, and Buying.* Routledge, 2019.

Kim, W. Chan., and Renée Mauborgne. *Blue Ocean Strategy: How to Create Uncontested Market Space and Make the Competition Irrelevant.* Boston, Massachusetts: Harvard Bus Review Press, 2016.

Krug, Steve. *Don't Make Me Think!: Web & Mobile Usability* - Das Intuitive Web. Heidelberg: Mitp, 2014.

Kylie, Cloris. *Beyond Influencer Marketing: Create Connections with Influential People to Build Authority, Grow Your List, and Boost Revenue.* Cloris Kylie LLC, 2018.

Levinson, Jay Conrad., and Ankie Blommesteijn. *Guerilla-marketing.* Amsterdam: Muntinga, 1990.

Loeffler, Bruce, and Brian Church. *Experience: The 5 Principles of Disney Service and Relationship Excellence.* Somerset: Wiley, 2015.

Lundstrom, Meg, and Charlene Belitz. *The Power of Flow.* New York: Random House, 1999.

Madison, Dan. *Process Mapping, Process Improvement, and Process Management: a Practical Guide to Enhancing Work and Information Flow.* Paton Press, 2008.

McKee, Robert, and Thomas Gerace. *Storynomics: Story-Driven Marketing in the Post-Advertising World.* Twelve, 2018.

Marr, Bernard. *Key Performance Indicators The 75 Measure Every Manager Needs to Know.* Pearson, 2012.

Martin, Karen, and Mike Osterling. *Value Stream Mapping: How to Visualize Work and Align Leadership for Organizational Transformation.* McGraw-Hill, 2014.

Mattson, David, and Brian W. Sullivan. Sandler *Enterprise Selling: Winning, Growing, and Retaining Major Accounts.* New York: McGraw-Hill, 2016.

McDonald, Jason. *SEO Fitness Workbook: The Seven Steps to Search Engine Optimization Success on Google.* JM Internet Group, 2019.

Meadows, Donella H., and Diana Wright. *Thinking in Systems: A Primer.* White River Junction, VT: Chelsea Green Publishing, 2015.

Mokalis, Alexa L., and Joel J. Davis. *Google Analytics Demystified.* Publisher Not Identified, 2018.

Murphy, Dallas. *The Fast Forward MBA in Marketing.* New York: John Wiley and Sons, 1997.

OBrien, Virginia. *The Fast Forward MBA in Business.* New York: Wiley, 1996.

Ogilvy, David. *Ogilvy on Advertising.* London: Prion, 2011.

Osterwalder, Alexander, Yves Pigneur, and Greg Bernarda. *Value Proposition Design: How to Create Products and Services Customers Want.* Wiley, 2015.

Paris, Joseph F. *State of Readiness: Operational Excellence as a Precursor to Becoming a High-Performance Organization.* Greenleaf Book Group Press, 2017.

Peppers, Don, and Martha Rogers. *Managing Customer Experience and Relationships: a Strategic Framework.* Wiley, 2017.

Peppers, Don, and Martha Rogers. *The One to One Future: Building Business Relationships One Customer at a Time.* London: Piatkus, 1993.

Peters, Thomas J., and Robert H. Waterman. *In Search of Excellence: Lessons from America's Best-run Companies.* New York: Harper & Row, 1982.

Popov, Linda Kavelin. *The Virtues Project: Simple Ways to Create a Culture of Character: Educator's Guide.* Austin, TX: Pro-Ed, 2000.

Porter, Michael E. *Competitive Strategy: Techniques for Analyzing Industries and Competitors.* New York: Free Press, 2004.

Pruitt, John, and Tamara Adlin. *The Essential Persona Lifecycle: Your Guide to Building and Using Personas.* Morgan Kaufmann, 2010.

Rackham, Neil. *Spin Selling*. McGraw Hill Book Company, 1988.

Revella, Adele. *Buyer Personas: How to Gain Insight into Your Customer's Expectations, Align Your Marketing Strategies, and Win More Business.* John Wiley & Sons, 2015.

Ries, Al, and Jack Trout. *Positioning: The Battle for Your Mind.* Beijing: Ji Xie Gong Ye Chu Ban She, 2016.

Rossman, J. Robert, and Mathew D. Duerden. *Designing Experiences.* Columbia University Press, 2019.Scott, David Meerman. *The New Rules of Marketing and PR: How to Use News Releases, Blogs, Podcasts, Viral Marketing and Online Media to Reach Your Buyers Directly.* Hoboken, NJ: J. Wiley & Sons, 2010.

Senge, Peter M. *The Fifth Discipline: The Art and Practice of the Learning Organization.* New York: Doubleday, 1990.

Simmons, Annette. *Whoever Tells the Best Story Wins: How to Use Your Own Stories to Communicate with Power and Impact.* New York: AMACOM, 2015.

Sinek, Simon. *Start with Why: How Great Leaders Inspire Everyone to Take Action.* Penguin Business, 2019.

Slywotzky, Adrian J. *The Art of Profitability.* New York: Warner, 2004.

Stawicki, Michal. *Making Business Connections That Count: the Gimmick-Free Guide to Authentic Online Relationships with Influencers and Followers.* Michal Stawicki, 2016.

Thirteenvirtues.com. Accessed September 08, 2018.
http://www.thirteenvirtues.com/

Underhill, Paco. *Why We Buy: The Science of Shopping; Updated and Revised for the Internet, the Global Consumer and Beyond.* Simon & Schuster, 2009.

Usborne, Nick. *Net Words: Creating High-impact Online Copy.* New York: McGraw-Hil Ventura, Michael P. Applied Empathy: the New

Ventura, Michael P. *Applied Empathy: The New Language of Leadership.* Hodder & Stoughton, 2019.

Vogl, Charles H. "Art Of Community: Seven Principles for Belonging." Readhowyouwant, 2016.

Walcoff, Philip. *The Fast Forward MBA in Business Planning for Growth.* New York: John Wiley, 1999.

Watkinson, Matt. *The Ten Principles Behind Great Customer Experiences.* Pearson, 2013.

Watson, David L., and Roland G. Tharp. *Self-directed Behavior: Self-modification for Personal Adjustment.* Australia: Wadsworth/Thomson Learning, 2001.

Warner, Mark. *Sales Funnel Management for Small Business* Owners. Independent, 2019.

Wickman, Gino. Traction *Get A Grip On Your Business.* Benbella Books, 2012.

Willeford, Dean. *Referrals And...: Recommendations, Introductions, Endorsements, Testimonials, Reviews, and Word of Mouth.* Create Space, 2014.

Witty, Adam, and Rusty Shelton. *Authority Marketing: How to Leverage 7 Pillars of Thought Leadership to Make Competition Irrelevant.* ForbesBooks, 2018.

Weinstein, Art. *Handbook of Market Segmentation: Strategic Targeting for Business and Technology Firms,* Third Edition. Hoboken: Taylor and Francis, 2013.

Wheeler, Alina. *Designing Brand Identity: An Essential Guide for the Entire Branding Team.* Wiley, 2018.

Wilhelm, Kevin. *Making Sustainability Stick: The Blueprint for Successful Implementation.* Pearson Education, 2015.

Williams, Roy H. *The Wizard of Ads: Turning Words into Magic and Dreamers into Millionaires.* Austin, TX: Bard Press, 1998.

Wright, Wallace. *Learning Systems Thinking.* Self-Published, 2019.

Zander, Robin Peter. *Responsive What It Takes to Create a Thriving Organization.* Create Space, 2017.

www.ingramcontent.com/pod-product-compliance
Lightning Source LLC
Chambersburg PA
CBHW071202210326
41597CB00016B/1639